MARCO ⊕ POLO

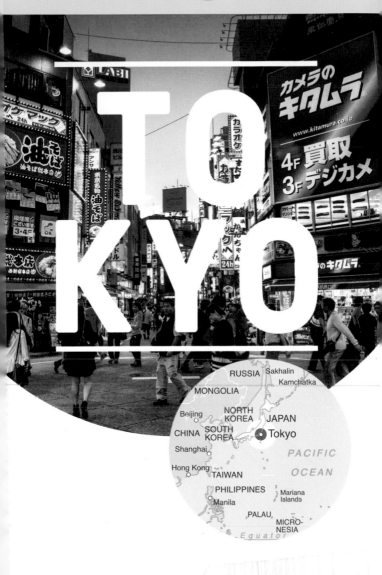

TO KYO

RUSSIA Sakhalin
MONGOLIA   Kamchatka
        NORTH
        KOREA JAPAN
Beijing
CHINA SOUTH   ● Tokyo
       KOREA
Shanghai   PACIFIC
Hong Kong   OCEAN
       TAIWAN
       PHILIPPINES Mariana
                    Islands
       ● Manila
            PALAU MICRO-
                   NESIA
          Equator

THE TOURING APP

shows you the way...
including routes and offline maps!

GET MORE OUT OF YOUR MARCO POLO GUIDE

IT'S AS SIMPLE AS THIS

1 go.marco-polo.com/tok

2 download and discover

GO!

WORKS OFFLINE!

SYMBOLS

INSIDER TIP Insider Tip
★ Highlight
●●●● Best of ...
≈ Scenic View
♲ Responsible travel: for ecological or fair trade aspects
(*) Premium-rate telephone numbers

PRICE CATEGORIES HOTELS

Expensive	over 25,000 yen
Moderate	15,000– 25,000 yen
Budget	under 15,000 yen

Prices are for two people in a double room with breakfast

PRICE CATEGORIES RESTAURANTS

Expensive	over 6,000 yen
Moderate	2,500– 6,000 yen
Budget	under 2,500 yen

Prices are for a starter and a main course, without drinks

CONTENTS

Ignatius
Church
Shinjuku-dōri
National
Theater
w Otani
seum
yama-dōri
Hie
Shrine
Uchibori-dōri
Chiyoda-ku
Imperial
Palace
Tōkyō
Station
Uchibori-dōri
National
Diet Bldg.
Sakurada-dōri
Atago-dōri
Inner Circular

DID YOU KNOW
Shrines and temples → p. 48
Giants vs. Swallows → p. 55
Fit in the city → p. 58
Gourmet restaurants → p. 64
For bookworms and
film buffs → p. 66
Specialities → p. 68
Business cards → p. 80
Time to chill → p. 90
Luxury hotels → p. 96
Currency converter → p. 119
Budgeting → p. 123

MAPS IN THE GUIDEBOOK
(130 A1) Page numbers and
coordinates refer to the street
atlas and the general map of
Tokyo and surrounding area
on p. 138/139
Coordinates are also given for
places that are not marked
on the street atlas
(0) Site/address located off
the map

(🗺 A–B 2–3) refers to the
removable pull-out map
(🗺 a–b 2–3) refers to the
additional inset map on the
pull-out map

INSIDE FRONT COVER:
The best Highlights

INSIDE BACK COVER:
Plan of Tokyo railway network

The best MARCO POLO Insider Tips

Our top 15 Insider Tips

INSIDER TIP **Clash of the heavyweights**
A sumo tournament is a one-of-a-kind experience. If you'd like to learn more about this sport, rent an *audio guide*. The "little voice in your ear" will comment on the match in English. (photo, right) → **p. 25**

INSIDER TIP **Creative epicentre**
One of the coolest neighbourhoods in the world for street style: in the labyrinth of *Shimokitazawa*, Tokyo is young, chaotic and creative → **p. 47**

INSIDER TIP **Cherry blossoms by night**
Even the most rational of people will go into raptures when they stroll among the beautifully illuminated trees along the *moat* of the Imperial Palace during cherry blossom season → **p. 31**

INSIDER TIP **Under the tracks**
Modern handicrafts with flair: the small shopping street *2k540 Aki-Oka Artisan* is the perfect place to find unusual souvenirs → **p. 81**

INSIDER TIP **High-priced dining in style**
Tōfuya Ukai serves tofu delicacies in a 200-year-old sake brewery; or you can enjoy your meal in the lovely garden → **p. 68**

INSIDER TIP **Eco-friendly Tokyo**
In the *Yoyogi Village* shopping complex you can find "green" products and organic restaurants. The light, modern architecture amid a plant-filled setting creates the perfect atmosphere → **p. 76**

INSIDER TIP **Rural paradise**
A stroll through the *Japan Open Air Folk House Museum* is like taking a walk through time and space → **p. 57**

INSIDER TIP **Expedition on two wheels**
Save your taxi fares and have fun: the best way to explore Kamakura – Japan's historic capital – by bicycle → **p. 58**

INSIDER TIP Seven, five and three in kimonos

Have your camera ready on 15 November, when girls and boys in these age groups put on their best outfits and visit shrines for the *Shichi-go-san* festival → **p. 115**

INSIDER TIP Everything for the kitchen

In the *Kappabashi* shopping street, you can find everything you need for cooking at low prices – from pans to wooden spoons to razor-sharp knives → **p. 76**

INSIDER TIP Relax at the pub

Everyone from students to office workers likes to sit together in *Man-maya* – an old farmhouse – and enjoy a beer or a rice wine → **p. 65**

INSIDER TIP Mysterious attraction

Legend has it that after dark you can discover which of Kawagoe's *Gohyaku Rakan Statues* looks most like you. There are over 500 statues in these temple grounds → **p. 59**

INSIDER TIP Great fun for techno-lovers

Throbbing with life at the weekends, *Womb* is home to Tokyo's best techno parties, where brilliant DJs keep the music playing along to spectacular dance floor laser shows → **p. 88**

INSIDER TIP Sumptuous blossoms at the shrine

In the original district of Nezu, people have prayed to the Shinto gods at this eponymous shrine since 1706. In late April, the 3000 plus azalea bushes that surround the shrine are in full bloom – an occasion for a joyful celebration with music and dancing → **p. 48**

INSIDER TIP A futuristic ride

After dark is the best time to ride the fully automated *Yurikamome Line*. Take a seat in the first car! The front window will give you an unobstructed view for taking photographs (photo left) → **p. 108**

BEST OF ...

FOR FREE

● *A bird's eye view*
You'd better not be afraid of heights when you whizz up from ground level to the 45th floor in the express elevator of the Shinjuku *City Hall*. The observation deck offers a fantastic view of the city – and entrance is free → p. 46

● *Temple and shrine festivals*
As hardworking as Tokyo's residents are, they enjoy a celebration just as much. Several times a year, every temple and shrine observes Matsuri, often featuring elaborate costumes and portable shrines. A unique atmosphere and plenty of photo opportunities – and all free of charge: for example, at *Sanja-Matsuri, Sannō-Matsuri* or *Kanda-Matsuri* → p. 33, 41, 51

● *Pop culture at Yoyogi Park*
Skip the expensive tickets for fashion shows, pop concerts or avant-garde theatre and come to the square at the southeast corner of the *Yoyogi Park* to see mild-mannered citizens transformed into rock 'n' rollers or eccentrically dressed girls → p. 40

● *High tech on Odaiba*
Japan is known as a high-tech nation that loves innovation. At the *Panasonic Center*, electronics enthusiasts can try out the latest cameras, tour a futuristic residence or learn about new concepts for saving energy → p. 47

● *A cycling tour around the Imperial Palace*
Every Sunday (except in heavy rain) you can borrow one of 150 free bicycles and pedal past the *Imperial Palace* (Photo) → p. 52

● *The majestic Meiji Shrine*
Tokyo's most important Shinto holy site welcomes visitors into its peaceful atmosphere free of charge, from sunrise to sunset. You can also often witness traditional weddings at the *Meiji Shrine* → p. 37

●●●● Dots in guidebook refer to "Best of..." tips

● *Contrasts between old and new*

In Tokyo, it always pays to stray from the major shopping streets. You will suddenly find yourself in narrow alleyways where the clocks seem to tick more slowly. Take the time to discover this side of Japan's capital: meander, for example through the little streets of *Azabujuban*, in the shadow of Roppongi Hills → p. 43

● *Early mornings at the fish market*

In the land of sushi and sashimi, Tokyo's *fish market* is a hub of activity. Nowhere in the world does more fish change hands on a daily basis; nowhere else is the sushi so fresh and delicious. Even if you're not a morning person, you shouldn't miss this sunrise spectacle → p. 49

● *High tech in Akihabara*

The Japanese love technology and electronics, and the *Akihabara* district holds a magical attraction for them. The countless discount shops offer many innovations from the audio and video sector as well as seemingly forgotten technology. Manga and Anime fans will also find treasures here → p. 76

● *Asakusa – traditional Tokyo*

Geishas no longer trip through the streets of the old district; nevertheless, you can still catch a whiff of old Tokyo flair in the area around the *Asakusa Kannon Temple* (photo). Whether you purchase your most beautiful souvenir or sample traditional sweets in *Asakusa*, a few pleasant hours are guaranteed → p. 32

● *Shibuya Crossing*

Probably no other intersection has been photographed or filmed as often as the one in front of the Shibuya railway station. The bustle of the crowd must be experienced to be believed → p. 37

● *Luxury shopping*

The residents of Japan's capital are passionate shoppers, especially for brandname and status items – and they are happy to pay for it. Don't forget the elegant gift-wrapping! The best hunting grounds: *Omotesandō* and *Ginza* → p. 37, 46

ONLY IN

BEST OF ...

● **Sing karaoke**
When it's pouring outside, it's all the more fun to get together with friends and sing away the bad-weather blues. There's no need for stage fright – you can have your own private little room, for example, at the *Shidax Roppongi Club* → p. 88

● **At the historical museum**
Step back into the Edo period. Even though the *Edo-Tokyo Museum* may look like a fantastic, futuristic building from the outside, on the inside you can take an exciting journey through time and explore the history of the Japanese capital → p. 49

● **An underground shopping expedition**
Shopping with an umbrella is not so much fun. But in the underground passageways of the *Shinjuku* or *Tokyo-eki* railway stations, you can take an unburdened shopping stroll → pp. 44, 29

● **Kabuki theatre**
A Kabuki theatre performance can easily last several hours. Take advantage of a wet day and immerse yourself in a piece of Japanese cultural heritage at *Kabuki-za* → p. 23, 91

● **East Asian Art**
As long as the rainy day is not a Monday, you can spend several wonderful hours at the *Nezu Museum*, where you can gain an insight into East Asian art and culture. If the sun does come out, a walk through the museum's beautiful garden is well worth your while → p. 39

● **Under water**
The residents of the *aquarium* at *Tokyo Sea Life Park* certainly won't be fazed by a little water. Even if you've visited large aquariums before, this one is worth a visit – even when it's sunny (photo) → p. 113

RAIN

RELAX AND CHILL OUT
Take it easy and spoil yourself

● *Soak and relax*

Bathing culture is highly valued in Japan, and you too can enjoy marvellous relaxation with a visit to a hot spring (*onsen*). After an intensive body cleansing ritual at the *Take-no-Yu Onsen*, you can relax in hot pools or tubs → **p. 90**

● *A green oasis in the city*

In the huge expanses of *Shinjuku Gyoen* park, you are guaranteed to find tranquillity. Alternatively, you can also sit on a park bench and enjoy the view of Shinjuku's skyscrapers while planning your next urban adventure → **p. 46**

● *Meditation and matcha tea*

A perpetually green bamboo grove, a rippling waterfall and a few treats accompanied by a bowl of matcha tea – at the *Hōkokuji* Temple in Kamakura, it's easy to lapse into meditation → **p. 58**

● *Culture and culinary pleasures*

Lean back in your seat in the large theatre at the *Bunkamura* Cultural Centre and enjoy an outstanding concert or ballet performance. After the show, you can dine on Japanese or Chinese cuisine on the top floor of the building → **p. 88**

● *The art of the tea ceremony*

At the historic *Imperial Hotel*, you can receive an introduction to the complicated ritual of the tea ceremony. The ceremony requires great concentration and precision on the part of the person performing it; for you, it calls for the ability to sit still and observe closely → **p. 92**

● *A feast for the senses*

At the gourmet restaurant *Kinsui*, everything is simply perfect. Located in the beautiful Chinzansō Garden, it offers premiere Japanese culinary culture. Savour every bite of the widely varied Kaiseki menu and delight in the aesthetic arrangement of little bowls and plates → **p. 64**

INTRODUCTION

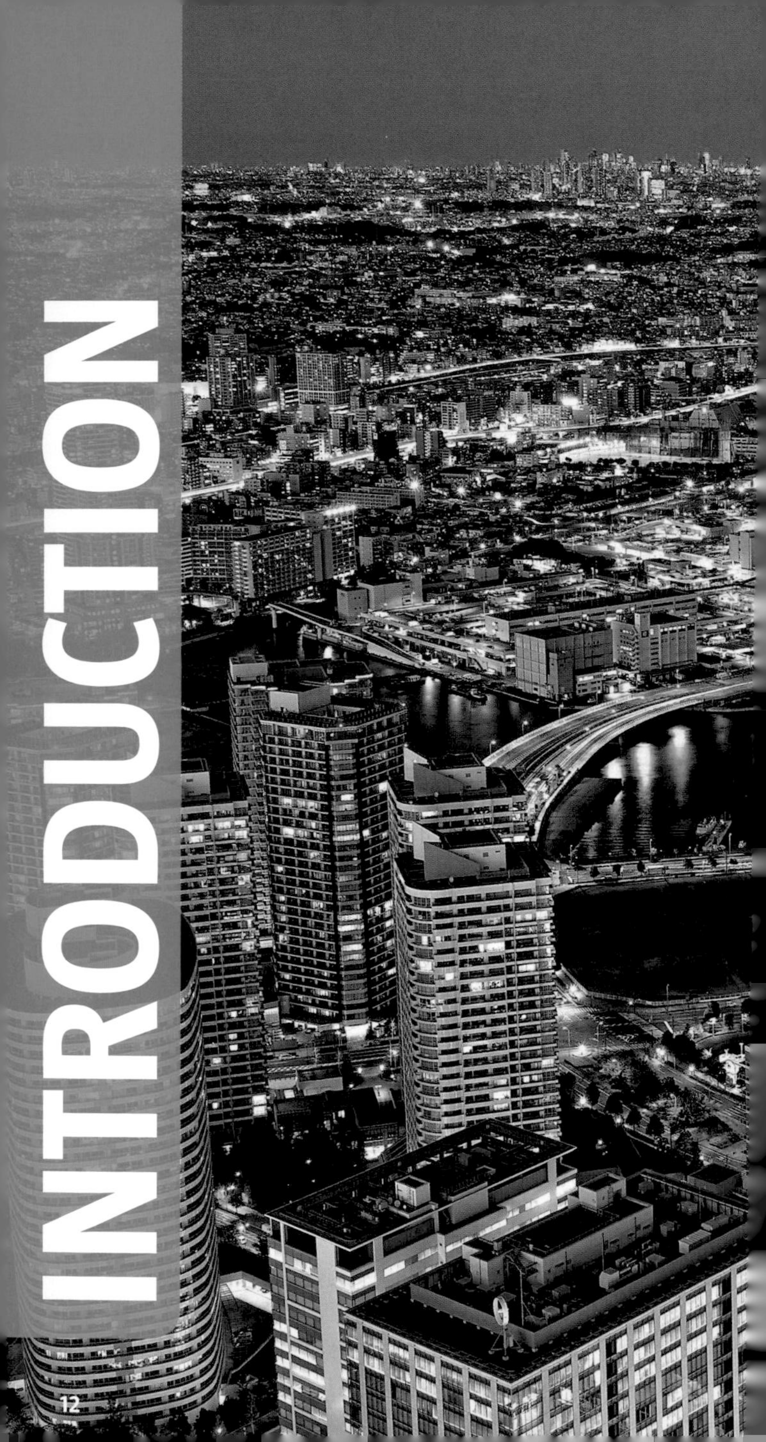

DISCOVER TOKYO!

Dynamic, gracious, a juggernaut, a collection of villages, exciting, provincial, ugly, exotic, stiff, vibrant... Choose any one of the characteristics from this list and put "Tokyo is..." in front of it and you've just made a true statement about Japan's capital. This city has such an endless number of different facets that it's unlikely anyone could ever reduce them to a common denominator. Starting at five o'clock every morning, the *largest fish market in the world* is a law unto itself when hundreds of gigantic tuna are auctioned off. Beginning around eleven, well-heeled, brand-conscious fashionistas traverse the elegant shopping strips, while gadget fans go hunting in the *hip electronics shops*. The traditions of old Japan live on in the Kabuki and Noh theatres, just as they do in the sandy ring of the sumo arena.

It will hit you at the latest at sunset, the so-called blue hour, when you look out from the *observation deck of a skyscraper*. As you survey the largest city in the industrialised world – this endlessly stretching metropolis with, to the west, the majestic volcanic cone of scared Mount Fuji towering over it – you will realise that this is a place where you can never be bored.

Photo: View of the harbour and the city

Tokyo is an adventure – a fascinating journey between the past and the future. But what is the best way to get to know this *dynamic megacity* with its constant desire for change? A simple way to get an initial overview is to board the *Yamanote Railway Loop*. Using Tokyo's most important transport connection, you have easy access to most of the major attractions. Pure travel time around the entire loop amounts to just 60 minutes; however, depending on your stamina levels and your desire to explore, you could easily be out and about all day long if you want to keep getting on and off. But don't get out of bed too early: you won't be doing yourself a favour. During the morning rush hour from 7.30 to 10am, Tokyo's trains are always extremely full.

The best place to start your city tour is on the Omotesandō in Harajuku – the *"Champs-Élysées" of Tokyo* – lined with stately trees and designer shops. On this luxurious boulevard and its small side streets the Far Eastern metropolis seems the most European. After wandering through the fashionable shops, climb aboard the Yamanote train. For a while, you will still be able to see the high treetops of the park surrounding the Meiji shrine; later, the *avant-garde skyscrapers* of Shinjuku dominate the panorama. The highest of these is the City Hall, the seat of Tokyo's governor. The gigantic city's numbers speak for themselves: over nine million people live in Tokyo's 23 city districts *(ku)* alone; including the incorporated cities and islands, there are approximately 13.5 million residents. Altogether, this amounts to approximately eleven percent of Japan's total population. The greater Tokyo area, including Yokohama, is home to more than 37 million people.

> **The metropolis feels most European on the Omotesandō.**

A colourful festival at the Meiji shrine: Dancing and drumming in traditional costumes

Riding the Yamanote railway, you will soon reach Takadanobaba station. Two of the most prestigious universities are located in this neighbourhood: Waseda and Gakushūin. *Emperor Akihito* studied at the latter, as did his two sons. "Ikebukuro!" the voice on the loudspeaker announces. The *60-storey shopping and recreation complex* Sunshine City towers above this modern section of the capital. It stands on historic ground: this was once the site of the Sugamo Prison, where war criminals from the Second World War were imprisoned; the accused were executed on 23 December 1948.

> **The world's largest fish market**

"Komagome", announces the conductor, "Tabata", "Nippori" and "Uguisudani". In English, these words mean something like "paddock of horses", "edge of a rice field", *"sunset village" and "nightingale valley"* – poetic names from a long-ago time; the reality looks very different. Today, the train glides past monotonous rows of houses. If it moved a little more slowly, you could catch a glimpse of the living conditions of the average Japanese citizen: mostly rather dreary settings, as the *flats are tiny*, without any special amenities – and expensive on top of that. Back to the horse paddock and the valley of nightingales: assuming you were to get out at one of these stations and walk around a bit, even a newcomer to Tokyo would notice the difference between this neighbourhood and an area like Shinjuku or your starting point, Omotesandō. Here it's more primal, more "in your face" and unadorned – the ugly along with the beautiful.

Somewhere in this part of the city runs an imaginary border, one that has always

divided Tokyo into two sections – into *Yamanote*, the upper city, and *Shitamachi*, the lower city of the underclass. The next station is called Ueno. If you get off here, you will be right in the heart of the former city centre. On a stroll through the narrow alleyways in the adjacent districts of *Yanaka and Nezu*, you will pass many temples and small shops and can still discover some elements of the old Tokyo. This is an appropriate moment to take a brief look at the city's eventful history. Viscount Ōta Dōkan is considered to be its founder. In the 15th century, he had a fortress built on the foundation walls of an old castle complex. However, the settlement that Tokugawa Ieyasu, ruler of the eight Kanto provinces discovered here over a century later could scarcely be called a "city". The community, which amounted to no more than 100 houses in total, was known as *Edo – gateway to the river*. Nevertheless, due to its strategically advantageous location, the warlord decided to establish his military headquarters here.

Another ten years went by, and the situation changed abruptly once again. In 1600, in the *Battle of Sekigahara*, Ieyasu defeated his princely rivals and in 1603 was declared Shōgun, the highest-ranking military ruler. The emperor – who had neither power nor influence – continued to reside in Kyoto. From this time on, policy was decided in Edo. The fishing village evolved into a metropolis. Beginning in 1634, all the feudal lords were required to assemble in Edo every other year, together with their complete retinues. Their families had to stay in Edo in any case – as hostages.

Old Japan lives on in the Kabuki and Noh Theatres.

Their residences lay to the south and west of the castle – in Yamanote. The simple people lived to the north and east – in Shitamachi. While the nobility led a regimented existence, urban culture blossomed here.

Beginning in the mid-19th century, the power of the Tokugawa shogunate declined. The "black ships" sailed into the bay near Edo led by the American Commodore Perry, who sought entry into a *nation that had been isolated for over 200 years*. With Emperor Mutsuhito's ascent to the throne in 1867, a new era began: the last shōgun was removed from power, and Edo became Tokyo, the "eastern capital", as the emperor had moved his residence here. The fundamental reforms that took place during his reign – which became known as the "Meiji Era" – paved the way for Japan's rapid industrialisation.

Back to the Yamanote tour: from Ueno, it is only a few stops to Tokyoeki, the *city's bustling main station*. From here, you're very close to the Marunouchi commercial district. Still, on some days you can feel the *sea air* through the open doors of the train cars – it can happen in this area when the winds are right. It is too easy to forget that Tokyo is a port city, and that the waterways were once its lifeline.

Even during the Edo Period, city planners began extending the capital toward Tokyo Bay. With gradual expansion work beginning in the mid-19th century, the small island fortresses were transformed into gigantic artificial land masses. On one of the islands, Odaiba, plans were made to construct a *City of the Future*. But when the speculative bubble burst in the early 1990s, city authorities were forced to rethink the project. As a result, large areas between the utopian-looking buildings remained free for parks, promenades and even a sandy beach. Unfortunately, though, this has already changed again, thanks to the construction boom that began with the awarding of the *2020 Summer Olympic Games* to Tokyo.

The fully automated Yurikamome train travels from Shimbashi across the Rainbow Bridge (illuminated from sunset to midnight) to the manmade island of Odaiba. It's a journey to a completely different Tokyo – an exhilarating and bizarre mixture of leisure area and futuristic architecture.

At the beginning of this century, the *new high-rise neighbourhood* of Shiodome was constructed around Shimbashi station – with apartment buildings, hotels and many restaurants and shops. Three stations further on the Yamanote Loop, the next imposing structure awaits: Shinagawa Station, which is also a stopping point for the *high-speed Shinkansen bullet trains*. Further on, around the Gotanda, Meguro and Ebisu stations, the atmosphere is quite busy; the many *small shops, restaurants and cafés* are always filled. Before the Loop closes in Harajuku, where you started, you should

City of the future: In Ginza and everywhere, high-rise buildings stretch up to the sky.

definitely get off in Shibuya. The garishly lit, sound-filled commercial streets *pulsate with Tokyo's youth culture*: this is where the trends of tomorrow are born. Still haven't seen enough? Then simply wait at the famous *Shibuya Crossing* for several traffic light cycles and observe how thousands of people cross the street all at once on a green light. You can get a good look at the spectacle from the connecting walkway between the Yamanote line and the Keio-Inokashira line.

Hip electronic shops, elegant fashion miles

So that's Tokyo? By no means! The Yamanote line circles only a small section of the metropolitan area. You won't believe how much more there is to discover!

WHAT'S HOT

1 Craft Beer

Art in a bottle Do you fancy a citrus-flavoured yuzu beer? If you love unusual beers, both local and international, you'll be happy in Tokyo. The best atmosphere, particularly for ship lovers, is at *Dry Dock (3–25-10 Shimbashi | Minato-ku)*, located underneath the tracks of the Yamanote line. For pizza fans, *Devil Craft (Ishikawa Bldg. | 4–2-3 Nihonbashi-muromachi | Chuo-ku)* is a wicked pleasure, and *Popeye (2–18-7 Ryogoku | Sumidaku) (photo)* is already something of an institution.

2 Dream destination

France Not really a new trend, but an ongoing one: the Japanese people's love of France. Hardly a wedding takes place in Japan without a French menu. For many people, Paris is the city of their dreams. There's even a word in the Japanese language to describe the pain one feels when Paris turns out to be less romantic than one had hoped. Luckily, Tokyo offers a small consolation: the district of *Kagurazaka* has something of a French flair with its brasseries and wine bars.

3 All wrapped up

Environmental consciousness 🌐 A horror for environmentalists, a pleasure for packaging designers: there's nowhere else in the world where products are packed as artistically as they are in Japan. And when it rains, an additional transparent plastic cover is quickly slipped over the paper bag. Yet this is gradually changing. Trends such as *My hashi* ("my chopsticks") or *My baggu* ("my bag") are taking a stand against throwaway mentalities and packaging rubbish. There are small chopsticks that can be disassembled and carried in a practical case and some shops offer discounts at the cash desk when you bring your own shopping bag.

Eat smarter

Lists of additives For a long time, people with food intolerances had a difficult time in Japan. Until recently, the policy everywhere was to cook in the way that tradition demanded. Yet in recent years, more and more chefs have become more flexible; restaurants and hotels more often identify allergenic food products on their menus or offer a list of ingredients. You can find out whether your desired meal contains things such as wheat, milk or soy in soup restaurants like *Tokyo Soup Stock (1–5-25 Yotsuya | Shinjuku-ku)* or in shops from the designer chain *Muji (3–8-2 Marunouchi | Chiyoda-ku)*.

Under the bridge

Favourite pubs Space is rare and precious in the densely built city of Tokyo. Every free corner is put to use – even under railway bridges. Many pubs have opened up in these locations, referred to as *gado shita*, "under the girders". They are favourites among many of Tokyo's residents: always cramped, but with plenty of atmosphere, and often with makeshift tables and stools on the street out the front. If you walk between the Yurakuch and Shimbashi stations on the Yamanote Loop, you're sure to discover something – and you can experience what Tokyo was like in the Shōwa period (1926–1989). Despite their enthusiasm for everything modern, the *gado shita*, which have been around since the 1950s, are more beloved than ever among the people of Tokyo!

IN A NUTSHELL

CALENDAR

Up until 1945, the Japanese emperor (Tenno) was considered godlike. However, since the end of the Second World War, his responsibilities have been purely ceremonial, and he is not allowed to exert any influence over policy. Nevertheless, he does play a role in everyday life: for example, in the way dates are written. Each new emperor proclaims a new motto – for example, the Heisei Era ("peace everywhere") under Akihito. This emperor ascended the throne in 1989, the year the Japanese call Heisei 1. Twice a year, on 23 December, Akihito's birthday, and on 2 January, he appears several times a day with his family members on the balcony of the Imperial Palace in Tokyo, before thousands of visitors.

FUKUSHIMA

On the afternoon of 11 March 2011 (also known as 3/11), when the strongest earthquake on record shook Japan, no one suspected what devastating effects it would have. The Tōhuku earthquake, which measured 9.0 on the Richter scale, triggered a massive tsunami. The seismic wave raced across the north-eastern coast of the main island of Honshu and took the lives of nearly 20,000 people. It destroyed houses, streets, fields and nearly the entire eastern Japanese fishing fleet. In the province of Fukushima, a nuclear power plant was flooded; the consequences were disastrous. The reactors' power supply broke down completely, resulting in a meltdown with large quantities o

Tokyoites are masters of the balancing act between ancient rituals and the trendy, colourful culture of fun.

radioactivity being released. The Fukushima plant is located approximately 250 km/155 mi northeast of Tokyo. In the first weeks after the tsunami, radioactivity was detected in the air and water in Tokyo as well. On the seven-point scale that measures the perceived strength of earthquake tremors, Tokyo scored 5+. No houses collapsed but soil liquidation occured in the eastern city. Just a few months later, life in the metropolis was running normally again at a superficial level, despite temporary limitations on electricity usage. These island people, who have been plagued by earthquakes, volcanic eruptions and tsunamis since time immemorial, are well aware that nature cannot be controlled. Every year, hundreds of perceptible quakes rock the country; thus, the architecture is well adapted and emergency drills are practised regularly.

Nevertheless, Fukushima represented a break: in addition to most obvious consequences – the fact that hundreds of thousands of people had to flee the heavily contaminated region around the nuclear power plant and the area destroyed by the tsunami, losing all of their possessions; as well as the economic problems brought on by the disaster – what was difficult for many Japanese to bear was the feeling that they were no longer the nation that had mastered every form of technology.

GENDER EQUALITY

Japan is a male society. In leadership positions in politics and business, women are vastly underrepresented. In the World Economic Forum's "Gender Gap Report", which studies degrees of gender equality in approximately 140 countries, Japan trails far behind other industrialised nations, not even rank-

Kabuki theatre: In keeping with ancient tradition, even the female roles are played by men

Despite the Fukushima disaster, and even though hundreds of thousands of Japanese people were killed or injured by the atomic bomb attacks on Hiroshima and Nagasaki at the end of the Second World War, the nation – under a liberal democratic, corporate-friendly government – continues to rely on nuclear power. A phase-out is not in sight, as the power of the "nuclear village" – a clique made up of government representatives, power plant operators, scientists and the media – remains unbroken.

ing among the top 100. With its "Womenomics" initiative, the government has placed the promotion of women high on its agenda; up to now, however, it has not moved beyond lip service. Only a few women have been able to break through the "glass ceiling". Still, at least at the lower management level and in large and international companies, more and more women do not (have to) content themselves with administrative roles but are pursuing careers just like their male colleagues.

MANNERS

In Japan, there are specific rules of behaviour for nearly every situation. Many of these stem from a time when the society was still rigidly organised according to hierarchy. This is still reflected to a certain degree today in the working world, where recent university graduates rank at the very bottom of a company's internal hierarchy, and promotions are granted primarily on the basis of age rather than performance. For foreigners, Japanese etiquette is a closed book. Who is supposed to bow to whom when, and how low, is almost impossible to learn. But don't feel afraid of embarrassing yourself. The Japanese are very tolerant of *gaijin* (foreigners), and look beyond the many *faux pas* that every visitor unavoidably commits. Nevertheless, there are a few rules you should take to heart: eating, drinking or talking on the phone on public transport is frowned upon. Blowing one's nose loudly is also horrifying to the Japanese, and raising one's voice in indignation is embarrassing. On the other hand, slurping your noodle soup loudly is a sign that you are enjoying it.

NOH, KABUKI, ETC.

In Tokyo, you have the opportunity to familiarise yourself with all the forms of classical theatre: Noh, Bunraku and Kabuki. Noh theatre originated in the 13th century and was initially reserved for the aristocracy. All of the characters, including the female roles, are portrayed by men. The makeup, gestures and movements are stylised to the point of abstraction. The sequence of plays, which lasts for several hours, is broken up by Kyōgen, burlesque interludes in which the voice of the people is allowed to be heard.
Bunraku is a form of puppet theatre with nearly life-sized marionettes. As in Noh, the storyline is illuminated by the orchestra and one or more narrators.
● The third form, Kabuki theatre, dates from the 17th century. It consists of singing, pantomime and dance. The performers – again, exclusively male – are often expressively made up. The primary musical instrument is a stringed one, the shamisen.

OLYMPIA 2020

The announcement of the International Olympic Committee (IOC) decision in the summer of 2013 was met with tremendous cheers in Japan: in 2020, the Summer Olympic Games will take place in Tokyo for the second time – the first was in 1964. The old Olympic stadium in Shinjuku is being replaced by a modern one and most of the sport venues will be located in Tokyo Bay.

PACHINKO

The noise that emanates from the garishly coloured arcades is indescribable. Inside are the pinball-like machines where housewives, students, office workers and corporate executives seek "relaxation". Steel balls race up and down through a labyrinth of nails. Players can pass the time waiting for the clatter that announces a win by watching a miniature television above the game console. Monetary prizes are not allowed; players win chocolate or cigarettes, which can be traded at inconspicuous counters nearby.

POLITICS

Since the end of the Second World War, with very few exceptions, Japan's politics have been defined by the Liberal Democratic Party (LDP), regarded as corporate-friendly, conservative and nationalistic. At the domestic level, debates in parliament revolve around raising the value added tax, combatting deflation, new security laws and amending the pacifist post-war constitution. International politics are dominated by territorial disputes with the country's neighbours – South Korea, Taiwan, China and Russia – over various island groups. The fact that Japan has not come to terms with its role as the aggressor in the region before and during World War II continues to taint its relationships with its neighbour countries.

Since 2016, Tokyo has been governed by a woman for the first time. Yuriko Koike is the official governor of the capital; her responsibilities are comparable to those of a mayor. The LDP politician, who ran for one of Japan's most important offices against her party's wishes, wants to cut costs, and even reduced her own salary when she took office. Other items on her agenda include moving the Tsukiji Fish Market to a new location and preparing Tokyo for the 2020 Olympic Games.

PUSHING ETTIQUETTE

A newcomer to Tokyo who attempts to travel on the subway for the first time during rush hour will be likely to utter a gasp. First, because helplessly crammed in the mass of people, they will scarcely be able to breathe; and second, in reaction to the ruthless behaviour they will witness.

Japanese politeness is legendary; however, when millions of commuters from the suburbs make their way in or out of Tokyo's city centre, a different set of rules is in place. On the platform, everyone still dutifully queues up; but when it is time to board the already bursting cars, all consideration is thrown to the wind. Do as the natives do: if the train seems so full that no one more will fit, enter the car backwards and facing outward. If you speak, do so softly.

On some lines, certain compartments are reserved for women during rush hour, in order to spare them from the threatening crowds. Unwitting foreigners who wander into the cars marked with pink stickers are silently tolerated.

The rule of thumb for moving through overcrowded stations or hectic pedestrian crosswalks like Shibuya Crossing is this: simply walk straight ahead with your head lowered – or better still, with tunnel vision into the distance. Everyone does it this way, and oddly, this behaviour reduces the danger of collision significantly.

SILVER MARKET

The term "Silver Market" refers to the growing consumer share of Japan's senior citizens. Entire branches of industry have developed that specialise in the needs of the millions of retirement-age Japanese – definitely a lucrative market. One quarter of all Japanese citizens are over 65. With the lifetime average number of births per woman at 1.4, Japan's birth rate is among the lowest in the world. Despite the fact that Japan has long lamented its ageing society, politicians have provided very few incentives – in terms of childcare or financial support – that might raise the birth rate. Instead, prestigious kindergartens – with which the rigorous career of a Japanese child begins – and preparations for entrance exams for the most highly regarded schools cost a small fortune.

SUMO

While younger Japanese people enjoy baseball games, the older generation prefers the national sport of sumo wrestling. In this 1500-year-old sport, two wrestlers – each weighing well over 100 kg/220 lbs – face off and flex their muscles in matches that often last only a few seconds. In recent years, sumo's image has suffered due to various scandals involving bribery, alcohol and connections to the Japanese mafia. Furthermore, most of the top wrestlers come from Mongolia and Eastern Europe. Still, it continues to be very popular, and a tournament is quite an experience! Two-week-long Grand Sumo Tournaments are held in January, May and September in Tokyo's Kokugikan Hall in

TRENDSETTERS

Young Tokyoites – especially the *joshi kōsei*, high school girls – create and dictate nearly all of the trends and passing fads in Japan. Only a few of them are lasting, but one guiding principle has dominated for a long time: it's got to be *kawaii* – cute, that is. Reactions

Trends are replacing traditions: Geishas are seen in public less and less frequently.

the Ryōgoku district. Day passes are available at the booths in front of the main entrance *(www.sumo.or.jp/en/index)*. It is best to purchase tickets at the beginning of the week and as early as possible: get in line by 7am. Once you have your tickets, you can go out for breakfast or visit the nearby Edo-Tokyo Museum as the most interesting matches begin around 2-3pm. It is worth hiring an INSIDER TIP audio device that broadcasts English-language commentary by a knowledgeable announcer. These are available at the entrance hall.

among the older generation range from surprise to shock; some even have their doubts about the nation's continued existence. But it's just the same as everywhere else – there's a need for fun. It's simply more noticeable in Japan – a society in which the group is traditionally placed before the individual. Still, there are negative spin-offs, such as *enkō* – online dating services that broker prostitution by schoolgirls, who hope to earn enough money to cover the costs of their fashionable outfits.

SIGHTSEEING

WHERE TO START?
CITY
Shibuya Station (134 B4)
(⌁ F10): In the gigantic city of Tokyo, it can be a hard to know where
to start exploring, as there's no real
city centre. However, if you wish to
experience the traditional and the
modern in one small area, Shibuya
is a good choice. The district is
shaped as much by the shopping
cult of the teenagers and young people and the teeming masses around
Shibuya Crossing as it is by the city's
largest Shinto sanctuary, the Meiji
shrine. You can reach Shibuya Station by subway (Z 01, G 01, F 16) or
suburban railway (Yamanote).

Tokyo is like a mosaic with a few large stones and countless smaller ones.
How you piece the picture together is
up to you.

You can check the "must-sees" off your
list relatively quickly, yet there will still
be an endless number of things to see:
the beautiful and the strange, the historic and the hypermodern. In the course of
your wanderings, you'll discover more
shrines, temples, monuments and other things than any travel guide can list –
little things that may not be considered
important, but which for many people
represent the true attractions of the Japanese capital.

They don't stand out immediately; they
wait to be discovered between the skyscrapers, utility poles and garish bill-

Hyper-modernism and classical culture: From architecture fans to Zen romanticists, there's something for every taste

boards. The Japanese have mastered this art of selective observation perfectly. It's the important things that matter: the tip of an elegantly curving temple roof that nearly covers up a building site fence; the delicate window screen of a dilapidated wooden house; a postmodern glass and marble building between garages made of corrugated steel.

Almost nothing is left of the historic substance of the old imperial city: fires, earthquakes and the bombs of the Second World War have destroyed most of it.

Of course, a visit to a museum provides a direct route to the enjoyment of art with Tokyo's museums focussing primarily on Asian – and here, particularly Japanese – art. Whether it's Zen painting or calligraphy, Chinese porcelain or modern Japanese ceramics, decorative kimonos or classical Japanese woodcuts, or even indigenous folk art: the variety is overwhelming. Museums are generally closed on Mondays and during the public New Year holidays, as well as when exhibitions are being changed. Entrance

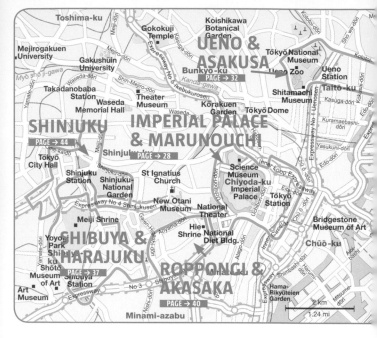

This map shows the locations of the most interesting city districts. For each district, you will find a detailed map identifying all the highlights described here by number.

fees for special exhibitions are higher than those listed here.

One more tip: focus mainly on Japanese art. You'll have your work cut out to take everything in!

IMPERIAL PALACE & MARUNOUCHI

The country's most powerful people gather around the emperor, who fulfils his duties as the highest-ranking Shinto priest and "symbol of the people", surrounded by his court officials.

On the one hand, these "powerful people" are Japan's politicians – in parliament and members' offices. The others are in the business district of *Marunouchi*, in Japan's top corporations and media companies.

■ CENTRAL RAILWAY STATION
(東京駅 (赤煉瓦の駅舎))
(136 C1) (*ﬃ O7*)

Kingo Tatsuno modelled Tokyo Station *(Tokyo-eki)*, constructed in 1914, on Amsterdam's Central Station. The building was heavily damaged by American air strikes in 1945, but extensive renovations on the Marunouchi side have restored much of its original charm.

Venture into the hustle and bustle. All of the capital city's major railway stations

SIGHTSEEING

are something to be experienced – and the *Tokyo-eki* most of all: the masses of humanity during rush hour, the ● kilometres of underground shopping tunnels on the Yaesu side of the station – this is where you can take a crash course in big city life. *Subway M 17 Tokyo | Yamanote loop line Tokyo*

2 IDEMITSU MUSEUM OF ART
(出光美術館) (136 B2) (*ⓜ N8*)

One of the largest private museums in Tokyo, with the world's largest collection of ink paintings and calligraphy works by the Zen monk Sengai (1750–1837). Woodcuts and genre paintings by important artists offer a glimpse into the long-lost world in the entertainment districts of Edo and Kyoto. The main hall contains a valuable collection of Chinese and Japanese ceramics. *Tue–Sun 10am–5pm, Fri until 7pm | Admission ¥1000| Teigeki Bldg. 9F | 3–1-1 Marunouchi | 3–1-1 丸の内 | Chiyoda-ku | 千*

代田区 | *www.idemitsu.com/museum/honkan/index.html | U-Bahn H 07, C 09 Hibiya*

3 INSIDER TIP INTERMEDIATHEQUE
(インターメディアテク)
(136 C1) (*ⓜ O7*)

In 2013, the 38-storey JP Tower was constructed on the site of the old post office. Fortunately, the developers preserved a large portion of the original façade, designed in 1931. Two floors of the building are reserved for the Intermediatheque, an unusual museum that covers a range of topics from music to media to medicine. The frequently changing exhibitions are supplemented by film screenings and concerts. *Tue–Thu 11am–6 pm, Fri/Sat until 8 pm | Admission free | 2–7-2 Marunouchi | 2–7-2 丸の内 | JP Tower | Chiyoda-ku | 千代田区 | www.intermediatheque.jp/en | Subway M 17 Tokyo | Yamanote loop line Tokyo*

MARCO POLO HIGHLIGHTS

⭐ **Asakusa Kannon Temple**
Colourful hustle and bustle at the temple of the goddess of mercy → p. 33

⭐ **Kamakura**
The old capital city on the coast is rich in temples, gardens and shrines → p. 57

⭐ **Hamarikyū Garden**
A teahouse against a backdrop of skyscrapers: here, tradition and modernity stand side by side → p. 46

⭐ **Tokyo Skytree**
A magnificent view from the world's second-tallest building → p. 53

⭐ **National Museum**
An intensive course in Japanese cultural history → p. 33

⭐ **Meiji Shrine**
A space for contemplation in the hectic city centre → p. 37

⭐ **Yanaka & Nezu**
Districts filled with history and flair → p. 48

⭐ **Fuji-san**
Every summer, hundreds of thousands of pilgrims ascend Japan's sacred mountain – an unforgettable experience → p. 57

⭐ **Roppongi Hills**
A city within the city – a modern Tokyo landmark → p. 42

⭐ **Fish Market**
A grandiose spectacle at the world's largest fish market → p. 49

29

IMPERIAL PALACE & MARUNOUCHI

4 IMPERIAL PALACE (皇居)
(132 A–B 5–6, 136 A–B1)
(🛱 M–N 6–7)

The Imperial Palace and large parts of the palace grounds, which cover 110,000 m²/27 acres, are closed to the public. Only on the emperor's birthday (23 December) and on 2 January are the inner gardens open, and the royal family appears on the balcony. Otherwise, the only section open to the public is the East Garden, former site of the imposing Edo Castle, residence of the shōguns from 1603 to 1867.

But a walk along the palace walls is definitely worth the time: it leads past the massive walls and guardhouses dating from the Edo period and seemingly impenetrable gates such as the *Sakurada-mon* **(136 A–B1)** *(🛱 M7)*, the "cherry blossom field gate". The palace's *main entrance* **(136 A–B1)** *(🛱 N7)* is easily recognizable with its two bridges and the Fushimi Tower – one of three remaining original buildings of the old Edo Castle complex.

In the East Garden **(132 B5–6)** *(🛱 M–N6)*, the path leads to the Ōtemon, the perfectly preserved main gate of the Edo Castle, past an old guardhouse to the castle's main section, the Hon-no-maru. All that is left here are an old watchtower and the foundation of the once-mighty castle keep. Behind the keep, but no longer in the East Garden, lies Kitanomaru Park, home to the Budōkan martial arts hall, which hosted the Olympic judo competition in 1964 and is scheduled to do so again in 2020. At the edge of the park there are several museums, including the National Museum of Modern Art. If you're in Tokyo during cherry blossom season, be sure to stroll along the *Chidorigafuchi moat*,

Deceptive idyll with swan: Massive walls and a moat protect the Imperial Palace.

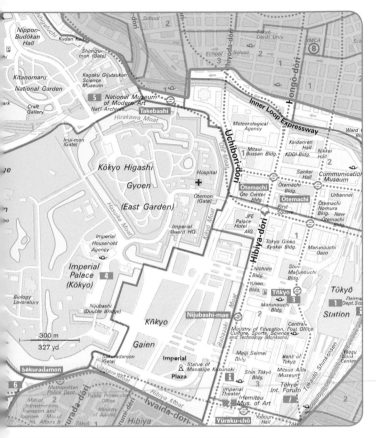

SIGHTSEEING AT THE IMPERIAL PALACE & MARUNOUCHI

1 Central Railway Station
2 Idemitsu Museum of Art
3 Intermediatheque
4 Imperial Palace
5 National Museum of Modern Art
6 Parliament
7 Tokyo International Forum

which is lined with hundreds of cherry trees. **INSIDER TIP** Particularly at night, when the trees are illuminated, the view is spectacularly beautiful. East Garden: *usually Tue–Thu, Sat, Sun 9am–4 or 5pm (irregular opening hours due to ceremonies) | 1–1 Chiyoda | 1–1 千代田 | Chiyoda-ku | 千代田区 | www.kunaicho.go.jp/eindex.html | Subway C 11, Z 08 Ōtemachi*

5 NATIONAL MUSEUM OF MODERN ART (東京国立近代美術館) (132 B5) (*∅ M–N5*)

Here you can get a good overview of the Japanese art scene of the 20th century. The section for arts and crafts is housed separately, in a neo-Gothic brick building. In the former headquarters of the Imperial Guard, constructed in 1910, Japa-

Plenty of atmosphere at the Sanja Festival in the Asakusa Shrine

nese ceramics, lacquer and metalwork, textiles and wickerwork are on display. *Tue–Sun 10am–5pm, Fri until 8pm | Admission ¥430 | 3–1 Kitanomaru Kōen | 3–1 北の丸公園 | Chiyoda-ku | 千代田 区 | www.momat.go.jp/english | Subway T 08 Takebashi*

⑥ PARLIAMENT (国会議事堂) (135 F1–2) (*Ⓜ L7–8*)

In the middle of the dreary-looking Kasumigaseki government district, the 201 m/ 660 ft-long Diet Building, completed in 1936, almost seems like a miracle of ingenuity. Possible references to the German monumental architecture of the same era may be coincidental. The tower above the main entrance is 65.5 m/215 ft high. Tours are possible outside of plenary sessions *(Mon–Fri 8am–5pm | www. sangiin.go.jp/eng/info/dbt/index. htm). 1–7-1 Nagata-cho | 1–7-1 永田町 | Chiyoda-ku | 千代田区 | Subway M 14, C 07 Kokkaigijidō-mae*

⑦ TOKYO INTERNATIONAL FORUM (東京国際フォーラム) (136 B–C1) (*Ⓜ O7*)

Opinions about this multipurpose facility containing concert halls, conference rooms, restaurants and shops range from "breathtakingly beautiful!" to "cold and forbidding". One thing is certain: despite its earthquake-proof steel construction, the 60 m/197 ft-high glass atrium is light and delicate. *3–5-1 Marunouchi | 3–5-1 丸の内 | Chiyoda-ku | 千代田区 | www.t-i-forum.co.jp/en | Yamanote loop line Yūrakuchō | Subway Y 18 Yūrakuchō*

UENO & ASAKUSA

● Asakusa, the district surrounding the Asakusa Temple, is the cradle of Edo culture. The red-light district of Yoshiwara with its courtesans and the actors from the Kabuki theatre are all things of the distant past.

later building, constructed in 1692, survived the Great Kantō earthquake of 1923, but not the bomb attacks of the Second World War. The reconstruction, made of reinforced concrete, was dedicated in 1958. To this day, the Sensōji is the centre of the former entertainment district of Asakusa. Even now, the close links of sacred function and wordly trade are clear to all the visitors who walk past the god of wind and thunder, through the massive southern gate Kaminarimon (Thunder Gate), under the huge red lantern, and enter the bustling shopping street of Nakamise that leads up to the Sensōji. The discovery of the little Kannon figure is celebrated twice each year (18 March and 18 October) with a magnificent golden dragon dance. *Summer: open daily 6am–5pm; Winter: 6:30am–5pm | 2–3-1 Asakusa | 2–3-1 浅草 | Taitō-ku | 台東区 | Subway G 19, A 18 Asakusa*

Yet even today, you can detect a hint of this atmosphere: for example, on a visit to the neighbourhood bath house, which is frequented by heavily tattooed *Yakuza* gangsters, or if you pass an old man in a cotton kimono on the street, politely greeting an Asakusa Geisha. In the adjacent district of *Ueno*, Japan's artistic treasures beckon from the National Museum. The present day cannot be ignored in either of these districts – homeless people have set up their plastic tarpaulin camps on the Sumida River.

■1 ASAKUSA-KANNON-TEMPLE (SENSOJI) (あさくさかんのん浅草寺) ★ (133 F2) (*ωω S1*)

Legend has it that in the year 628, two fishermen pulled a small statue of Kannon, the goddess of mercy, out of the Miyato River with their nets. After all attempts to return the figure to the water had failed, they delivered their mysterious discovery to their master. He immediately ordered a hall to be built – the predecessor to the present-day temple. The

■2 ASAKUSA SHRINE (ASAKUSA-JINJA) (浅草神社) (133 F2) (*ωω S1*)

This Shinto shrine is dedicated to the two fishermen and their master from the founding legend of the neighbouring Asakusa Kannon Temple. The Shrine Festival, held in May ● INSIDER TIP *Sanja-Matsuri*, is one of the city's most fascinating spectacles. *Open daily 6am–5pm | 2–3-1 Asakusa | 2–3-1 浅草 | Taitō-ku | 台東区 | Subway G 19, A 18 Asakusa*

■3 NATIONAL MUSEUM (東京国立博物館) ★ (133 D1) (*ωω P1*)

The National Museum ranks among the ten largest museums of Asian art worldwide. With close to two million visitors per year, it is also one of the most popular. Its sumptuous main building is devoted to treasures of Japanese art. Among the approximately 120,000 objects – primarily paintings, calligraphy, sculptures, textiles, ceramics, swords and armour –

87 have been classified as national treasures and an additional 634 as important pieces of cultural heritage. It would be impossible to display the entire inventory at one time; therefore, the objects are rotated several times per year. In addition, special exhibitions are held several times each year.

The adjacent building on the right, Toyōkan, focuses on the art of other Asian countries. Here, too, large special exhibitions are held frequently. The smallest and oldest building on the left – Hyōkeikan – houses archaeological artefacts from Japan. Along with pottery from the Middle Jōmon period (3500 to 2000 BCE), the most fascinating of these are the terracotta Haniwa figures – people, animals, houses and boats – which served as burial objects from the 3rd to the 7th centuries. At the time of printing, however, this building was closed for an indeterminate period for renovation.

Behind the Hyōkeikan stands the treasury of the Hōryūji Temple in Nara, a true jewel of an art space, which is treated with the appropriate care. In considera-

SIGHTSEEING IN UENO & ASAKUSA

1 Asakusa Kannon Temple (Sensōji)

The scent of old Edo: Creating a woodcut in the Shitamachi Museum

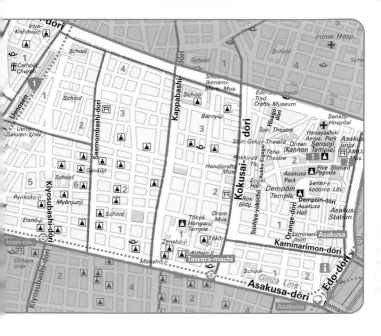

2 Asakusa Shrine (Asakusa-jinja)
3 National Museum
4 Shitamachi Museum
5 Tokyo Metrop. Museum of Art
6 Ueno Park

tion of the contents – objects over one thousand years old, many made of wood or paper – the building is only open to visitors on Thursdays. In case of rain, or when the humidity exceeds 70 percent, the treasury remains closed. *Tue–Sun 9:30am–5pm, longer for special exhibitions | Admission ¥620 | 13–9 Ueno Kōen | 13–9 上野公園 | Taitōku | 台東区 | www.tnm.jp | Subway G 16, H 17 Ueno | Yamanote loop line Ueno*

4 INSIDER TIP SHITAMACHI MUSEUM (下町風俗資料館) (132 C2) (*ℳ P2*)

If you don't manage to get a whiff of old Edo amid the sea of concrete buildings, it is worth taking a walk to this small black and white building on the southern edge of Ueno Park. Street scenes, glimpses into workshops, stores and living spaces, everyday utensils and photos from the time before the great earthquake of 1923 will help spark your imagination. *Tue–Sun 9:30am–4:30pm | Admission ¥300 | 2–1 Ueno Koen | 2–1 上野公園 | Taitōku | 台東 | www.taitocity.net/taito/shitamachi/english/index.html | Subway G 16, H 17 Ueno | Yamanote loop line Ueno*

5 TOKYO METROPOLITAN MUSEUM OF ART (東京都美術館) (132 C1) (*ℳ P1*)

The museum, which was renovated in 2012, frequently brings spectacular exhibitions to Tokyo thanks to co-operations with other heavyweights of the art world such as the Louvre. *Tue–Sun 9:30am–5pm | Admission varies according to exhibit | 8–36 Ueno Koen | 8–36 上野公園 | Taitō-ku | 台東区 | www. tobikan.jp | Subway G 16, H 17 Ueno | Yamanote loop line Ueno*

6 UENO-PARK (上野公園)
(132 –129 C–D 1–2) (ᗰ P1–2)

The statue of Takamori Saigō at the main entrance is a memorial to the bloody battle that took place here in May 1868. Un-

Shrine, the path to which is lined with many bronze and stone lanterns. In April, when the 1000 plus cherry trees are in bloom, the park overflows with visitors exuberantly celebrating *Sakura* – definitely something to experience!

Another lovely sight is always the collection of dolls at the feet of Kannon, the goddess of mercy at the *Kiyomizu Temple*: these are offerings from grateful parents whose wishes for children have been fulfilled. Every year on 25 September, the

Even during the cherry blossom season, it's still possible to find a quiet spot in Ueno Park

der Saigō's leadership, the last contingent of the Tokugawa shogunate was vanquished, paving the way for Japan's emergence as a modern nation.

One of the first results was Ueno Park itself. The new Meiji government had the former battlefield converted into a public park complex that had plenty to offer: in addition to numerous museums and concert halls, there is also the *Seiyōken* restaurant, which has been serving Western food since 1876, as well as the *Tōshōgū*

dolls are cremated in a solemn ceremony in order to make room for new offerings.

It is better to keep your distance from another goddess, Benten-sama, who resides in a temple on a small peninsula in Shinbazu Pond: driven by jealousy, she is said to have abruptly torn apart some tender bonds of love! *Always open | 5–20 Ueno Koen | 5–20 上野公園 | Taitō-ku | 台東区 | Subway G 16, H 17 Ueno | Yamanote loop line Ueno*

SHIBUYA & HARAJUKU

The districts of Shibuya and Harajuku are young, fashionable, chic and shrill. Yet even here you can find elements of traditional Japan: the Meiji shrine, whose main entrance is located just a few metres away from Harajuku Station, is Tokyo's most important Shinto sanctuary.

In Shibuya, on the other side of the most filmed and photographed street crossing in the world – ● Shibuya Crossing, with its swarms of people and enormous video screens – is the epicentre of Japan's youth culture. Hordes of high school girls populate this teenage wonderland – the consumer and entertainment paradise of the capital city's youth.

No one knows exactly where Harajuku – the district surrounding the suburban railway station of the same name – begins and ends. Harajuku stands for street fashion, creativity and flamboyant creations for the kids in the Takeshita-dōri. Directly adjacent, on Tokyo's luxury boulevard, ● Omotesandō, top international and Japanese designers convene. This is a favourite haunt of brand-conscious Tokyoites. The **INSIDER TIP** boulevard's side streets, where you can discover the small shops of young fashion designers, hairstylists, interior designers and restaurants are also very interesting. **INSIDER TIP** Cat Street, which branches off from Omotesandō and runs parallel to Meiji-dōri, has an atmosphere all its own, with colourful shops offering everything from knick-knacks to outdoor clothing.

■ HACHIKŌ (ハチ公)
(134 B4) (*Ⓜ F10*)

Where do you meet your friends in Shibuya? By Hachikō, of course – the bronze statue of an Akita dog. Hachikō was born in 1923 and belonged to a professor at Tokyo University. Every evening he appeared right on time at the same spot, to meet his master at the station. Even after the professor's death, Hachikō continued trotting to the same place at the familiar time, until ten years later he finally passed away himself. The monument already existed during the dog's lifetime, but it was melted down during the War. However, since 1948, Hachikō has been standing guard here once again, his faithful gaze directed toward the station's exit. *2–1 Dogenzaka* | *2–1 渋谷駅* | *Shibuya-ku* | *渋谷区* | *Subway G 01, Z 01, F 16 Shibuya* | *Yamanote loop line Shibuya*

■ MEIJI SHRINE (MEIJI-JINGŪ)
(明治神宮) ★ ●
(134 B1–2) (*Ⓜ E7–8*)

Scarcely any other building in Tokyo is as elegant and impressive as the Meiji Shrine. Consecrated in 1920, bombed in 1945 and rebuilt in 1958: the story of the shrine, which is dedicated to the Meiji emperor (1852–1912) and his wife Shōken (1850–1914), is short but eventful. It radiates as much tranquillity and dignity as if it had stood here for centuries. The shrine is also well protected: 100,000 bushes and trees shield it from the tumult of the city. Two gigantic *torii* – the first of these ceremonial gates is made of stone, the second of thousand-year-old cypress wood – span the wide gravel path.

To the right of the main hall, you can see countless small votive tablets hanging on trees and racks. It is not only Tokyoites who have immortalised their wishes for the future here. You can follow their example with confidence. Japan's Shinto gods are not daunted by language barriers!

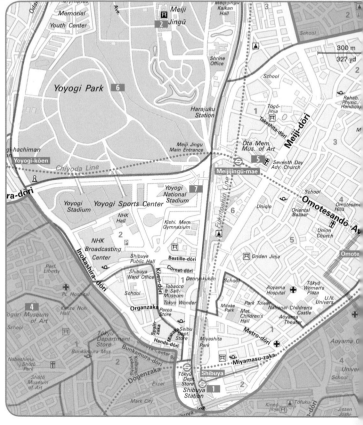

SIGHTSEEING IN SHIBUYA & HARAJUKU

1 Hachikō
2 Meiji shrine (Meiji-jingū)
3 Nezu Museum
4 Toguri Museum of Art
5 Ukiyo-e Ōta Memorial
Museum of Art
6 Yoyogi-Park
7 Yoyogi National Stadium

In May or June, if the irises are in bloom, a detour into the **INSIDER TIP** Iris Garden is worth your while. Empress Shōken also came here to take a break from the stresses of the monarchy. In the treasury located behind the shrine, objects from the estate of the royal couple are on display. Traditional ceremonies and festivals are often held at the Meiji shrine and these are definitely worth visiting. It's best to check the website for up-to-date schedules. *Shrine open daily 9am–4 pm, park from sunrise to sunset | 1–1-1 Yoyogi-ka-mizono-cho | 1–1-1 代々木神園町 | Shibuya-ku | 渋谷区 | www.meijijingu.or.jp/ english | Subway C 03, F 15 Meijijingūmae | Yamanote loop line Harajuku*

3 INSIDER TIP NEZU-MUSEUM
(根津美術館) ● (134 C3) (𝄞 H10)

A gem of a museum: the new building by Kengo Kuma, completed in 2009, puts the architectural cherry on top of this excellent private collection. The museum's founder, Nezu Kaichirō, began his collection at a time when Japan's former feudal lords were exchanging their artistic treasures for cash. He collected works by native artists as well as masterpieces from China and Korea. The museum's large garden is also worthy of a detour – it's a shady oasis in the big city, with a pond, stone lanterns and teahouses where tea ceremonies are also held. In the Nezu Café, seats by the windows with a view of the garden are particularly sought-after. *Tue–Sun 10am–5pm | Admission ¥1300| 6–5-1 Minami-Aoyama |* 6–5-1 南青山 *| Minato-ku |* 港区 *| www.nezu-muse.or.jp/en | Subway G 02, C 04, Z 02 Omotesandō*

4 TOGURI MUSEUM OF ART (戸栗
美術館) (134 A3–4) (𝄞 E10)

This massive building contains an exquisite collection of the finest porcelain from Japan, China and Korea. Tohru Toguri, the founder of the museum, assembled his collection of valuable objects over a period of 60 years. Upon request, the museum also offers INSIDER TIP private guided tours in English outside the official opening hours. The best part of these tours is that you get to hold the centuries-old exhibition pieces in your hands and observe them up close (make reservations three weeks ahead via e-mail: kouhou@ toguri.or.jp). Depending on the size of your group, it can cost up to £18/$25 per person – but it's worth it! Afterwards, you will look at porcelain and ceramics with different eyes. *Tue–Sun 10am–5pm | Admission ¥1000| 1–11-3 Shoto | 1–11-3* 松濤 *| Shibuya-ku |* 渋谷区 *| www.toguri-museum.or.jp/english | Subway Z 01,*

The gods are busy at the Meiji Shrine: Wooden tablets bearing wishes

G 01, F 16 Shibuya | Suburban railway Keio Inokashira Shinsen

5 UKIYO-E ŌTA MEMORIAL MUSEUM OF ART (浮世絵　太田記念美術館) (134 B2) (𝄞 F8)

The smaller the museum, the more you enjoy the art! This statement applies perfectly to the conveniently-located Ōta Museum, where you can admire Tokyo's largest and most beautiful collection of woodcuts (Ukiyo-e). The collection comprises over 12,000 woodcuts by masters such as Hiroshige (1797–1858) and Utamaro (1753–1806). It is supplemented by changing exhibitions based on various themes. A small stone garden with lanterns and a bench completes the cosy atmosphere and the tearoom on the lower level is an inviting place to take a break. *Tue–Sun 10:30am–5:30pm, irregular closing days; check calendar on the website | Admission ¥700–1000 | 1–10–10 Jingūmae | 1–10–10 神宮前 | Shibuya-ku | 渋谷区 | www.ukiyoe-ota-muse.jp/eng | Subway C 03, F 15 Meijijingūmae | Yamanote loop line Harajuku*

6 YOYOGI PARK (代々木公園) (134 A–B 1–2) (𝄞 E–F 7–8)

On weekends, the atmosphere at the former imperial army parade ground is vaguely reminiscent of New York's Central Park. From sunrise until after dark, this green space provides joggers, cyclists, musicians and acrobats with a place to practice or work out. Jugglers practise side-by-side with trumpet players; students rehearse on an imaginary stage; small dogs decked out in jackets and sunglasses trot along beside their proud owners. At the weekends, thousands of people look for a place to picnic and relax on the inviting meadow, bordered by cherry and maple trees. ● On Sundays, members of all kinds of subcultures gather at the southeast entrance and provide quirky subjects for photos: for example, rock 'n' roll dancers – the boys sporting quiffs and the girls in petticoats. Bring your camera! *Open round the clock | 2–1 Yoyogi-Kamizono-cho | 2–1 代々木神園町 | Shibuya-ku | 渋谷区 | Subway C 03, F 15 Meijijingūmae | Yamanote loop line Harajuku*

7 YOYOGI NATIONAL STADIUM (国立代々木競技場) (134 B3) (𝄞 E9)

On the site where the Americans built their quarters during the occupation period, the architect Kenzō Tange constructed two sports facilities for the 1964 Olympic Games. Today, the powerfully curving roofs of the two halls still appear both imposing and modern. *2–1–1 Jinnan | 2–1–1 神南 | Shibuya-ku | 渋谷区 | Subway C 03, F 15 Meijijingūmae | Yamanote loop line Harajuku*

ROPPONGI & AKASAKA

Nowhere else has Tokyo changed as rapidly as it has here. Up until a few years ago, Roppongi was known purely as an entertainment district, while the posh hotel district of Akasaka was beginning to lose its sparkle.

With the construction of the two high-rise complexes of Roppongi Hills and Tokyo Midtown, the future of urban development moved into these two districts – at least for the more affluent citizens. The concept is called "city in the city". There is plenty for art lovers to enjoy here as well, in the area known as the Tokyo Art Triangle, which includes the National Art Center, the Museum in Roppongi Hills and the Suntory Museum in Tokyo Midtown.

1 HIE SHRINE (HIE-JINJA)
(日枝神社) (135 F2) (*Ø L8*)

In the 15th century, the local ruler Ōta Dōkan had a shrine built here for Oyamakuni no kami, the tutelary deity of Edo. Under the patronage of the Tokugawa shoguns, it became Edo's most popular shrine; the shrine festival ● **INSIDERTIP** *Sannō-Matsuri* was known as the "unparalleled festival". It is still celebrated to this day in the middle of June. The highlight is the Shinto parade – a procession of portable shrines *(mikoshi)* in which approximately 300 people take part, wearing costumes in the style of the Heian period (9th to 12th centuries) – however, this only takes place in even-numbered years. Saying a prayer at the Hie shrine is said to protect against premature births and traffic accidents. However, the deity was less successful in protecting its own four walls as the shrine was reduced to rubble during the Second World War. In 1959, it was replaced by a new construction. *Sunrise–sunset | 2–10 5 Nagata-chō | 2–10 5 永田町 | Chiyoda-ku | 千代田区 | Subway G 05, M 13 Akasaka-mitsuke*

2 MORI ART MUSEUM
(森美術館) ⌁ (135 E4) (*Ø J10*)

The 53rd floor of the Mori Tower is a centre for unusual, sometimes provocative installations, videos and other contemporary forms of art. If you buy a ticket for the observation deck on the roof of the Mori Tower (approx. £10/$13.50), a visit to the museum is included. **INSIDERTIP** The best time to come is at sunset, when the lights are going on in Tokyo! *Wed–Mon 10am–10pm, Tue 10am–5 pm | Price of admission varies | 6–10-1 Roppongi | 6–10-1 六本木 | Minato-ku | 港区 | www.mori. art.museum/eng | Subway H 04, E 23 Roppongi*

3 THE NATIONAL ART CENTER, TOKYO (国立新美術館)
(135 D3) (*Ø J9*)

Behind the undulating façade designed by Kisho Kurokawa, the famous Japanese architect seems to have started running out of ideas, as the inside of the building – one of Japan's largest art centres –

Trendy: A sculpture by Takeshi Murakami at the Mori Art Museum

is rather sterile in appearance. However, this does not detract from the appeal of its changing exhibitions. If you need a rest, you can relax in one of the armchairs on the ground floor or in one of the centre's three cafés. *Wed–Mon 10am–6pm, Fri until 8pm | Free admission; exhibition prices vary | 7–22-2 Roppongi | 7–22-2 六本木 | Minato-ku | 港区 | www.nact.jp/ de/index.html | Subway C 05 Nogizaka*

SIGHTSEEING IN ROPPONGI & AKASAKA

1 Hie Shrine (Hie-jinja)

2 Mori Art Museum

3 The National Art Center, Tokyo

4 Nogi Shrine (Nogi-jinja)

5 Roppongi Hills

6 Tokyo Midtown

4 NOGI SHRINE (NOGI-JINJA)
(乃木神社) (135 E3) (∅ J9)

In 1912, when the casket of the Meiji emperor left the palace, the residents of this house committed *seppuku* – ritual suicide. The two people were General Nogi, a hero of the Russo-Japanese War, and his wife Shizuko. Ever since that time, Japanese visitors have felt magically drawn to this site – a simple building constructed in 1889 *(open daily 9am–4pm)*. The Nogi shrine located directly adjacent was built in honour of the cou-

ple and is very popular. It's clear architecture is particularly striking. *Daily 6am–5pm | 8-11-27 Akasaka | 8-11-27 赤坂 | Minato-ku | 港区 | Subway C 05 Nogizaka*

5 ROPPONGI HILLS (六本木ヒルズ) ★ (135 E4) (∅ J10)

"The city within the city" is a modern Tokyo landmark. The 116,000 m² / 1,250,000 sq ft city complex cost approximately 1.75 billion pounds/2.5 billion dollars. At the centre of the ambitious project is the 54-storey *Mori Tower* with its museum and observation deck. In addition, the "city" is home to over 200 shops and restaurants, a luxury hotel, four blocks of flats, a gigantic plaza that is often used for events, the headquarters of the Asahi television station and a cinema complex. Art objects – such as Louise Bourgeois' 10m/33 ft-high spider – and a Japanese garden provide additional variety and inspiration on a "city stroll" through Roppongi Hills. Here, too, you should definitely veer off a bit from the main shopping roads and wander through the small side streets in order to experience that contrast between old and new that is so typical of Tokyo. You will find that in the shadow of the glamourous boutiques and exclusive restaurants of Roppongi Hills – like those you can also find in New York – in the district of ● *Azabujuban*, there are still some little shops that specialise in lacquered wooden

shoes, *yukata* (cotton kimonos) or *tenugui* (traditional cotton towels). Out on the street, you can buy freshly-baked rice crackers or waffles filled with bean paste; in the winter there are steaming sweet potatoes cooked on mobile grills. Take a walk, and you are guaranteed to discover even more that is typically Japanese. *6–10-1 Roppongi | 6–10-1 六本木 | Mina-to-ku | 港区 | www.roppongihills.com/en | Subway H 04, E 23 Roppongi*

6 TOKYO MIDTOWN (東京ミッド タウン) (135 E3) (*∅ J–K9*)

In terms of height, the nearly 250 m/ 820 ft-high Midtown Tower, which opened in 2007, has overtaken the neighbouring Mori Tower in Roppongi Hills by just a few metres. The mega-complex, designed primarily by the US architectural firm Som, consists of six sections. On 53 storeys, they are home to shops and restaurants, offices and flats,

Enjoy a coffee in the curve after a full dose of art in the National Art Center

as well as the luxurious Ritz-Carlton Hotel. The *Suntory Museum of Art*, designed by Kengo Kuma, is worth a visit *(Wed–Mon 10am–6pm, Fri and Sat until 8pm | Admission varies according to exhibition)*. It displays Japanese art in changing exhibitions. The 21_21 Design Sight, created by architect Tadao Ando and fashion tsar Issey Miyake, is also impressive and often hosts design shows. *(Wed–Mon 10am–pm; closed 30 Dec–3 Jan | Admission ¥1100. 9–7-1 Akasaka | 9–7-1 赤坂 | Minato-ku | 港 区 | www.tokyo-midtown. com/en | Subway C 5 Nogizaka | Subway H 04, E 23 Roppongi*

Tallest skyscraper competition: The Tokyo Midtown mega-complex

SHINJUKU

A district of many facets: Shinjuku stands for shopping expeditions through department stores, duty free shops, trendy boutiques or the underground arcades in the labyrinthine ● Shinjuku Station. Shinjuku also encompasses the high-rise district to the west of the station, with its gigantic hotels and office buildings – and the city's most bizarre red light district, *Kabukichō*, to the station's northwest. The neighbourhood even offers something for nature lovers: the 58,000 m²/14 acre green space *Shinjuku Gyoen*.

1 BUNKA GAKUEN COSTUME MUSEUM (文化学園装飾博物館) (130 A6) (*∅ E6*)

This museum, which belongs to *Bunka Fashion College*, a famous fashion design school, contains a comprehensive collection of historic Japanese costumes from the Heian period up to everyday clothing from the modern era. Only a portion of the fabric artworks and unusual accessories is ever exhibited at one time. *Mon–Sat 10am–4:30pm | Admission ¥500 | 3–22-7 Yoyogi | 3–22-7 代々木 | Shibuya-ku | 渋谷区 | museum.bunka.ac.jp | Subway E 27 Shinjuku | Yamanote loop line Shinjuku*

2 NTT INTER COMMUNICATION CENTER (NTT コミュニケーションセンター) (130 A6) (*∅ D6*)

This interactive media art centre on the fourth floor of the 234 m/768 ft high Tokyo Opera City actually deserves a cooler name – as it is, the skyscraper's name refers to the new National Theatre that is housed here. Parts of the exhibition include sensational installations on the subjects of information and communica-

SIGHTSEEING

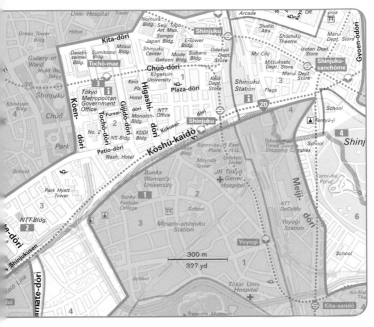

SIGHTSEEING IN SHINJUKU

1 Bunka Gak. Costume Museum
2 NTT Inter Comm. Center
3 City Hall (Tokyo Met. Building)
4 Shinjuku Gyoen

tion. The permanent exhibition contains high-tech art that you can touch, manipulate or simply wonder at. An electronic library with internet terminals and a cyber café complete this successful concept. Be sure to take plenty of time here: it's best to visit on weekday mornings, when the queues at the entrance are not too long. *Tue–Sun 11am–6pm | Admission varies according to exhibition | Tokyo Opera City Tower 4F | 3–20-2 Nishi-Shinjuku | 3–20-2 西新宿 | Shinjuku-ku | 新宿区 | www.ntticc.or.jp/index_e.html | Subway: light green Keiō New Line Hatsudai*

3 CITY HALL (TOKYO METROPOLITAN BUILDING) (東京都庁舎) ⚜ (130 A5) (𝄞 D–E5)

Monumental is probably the most accurate way to describe this 243 m/797 ft-high building made of granite and reinforced concrete. The legendary architect Kenzo Tange apparently wanted to create a monument to himself as well as to the Japanese capital with this edifice. The cost of building the world's tallest city hall was approximately 885 million pounds/1.25 billion US dollars. ● You can fly up to the observation decks on the 45th floors of the two towers in the express elevators – don't miss this opportunity for a free view of Tokyo! *Open daily 9:30am–11pm; closed 29 Dec–3 Jan and on inspection days (then only one tower is open until 11pm) | 2–8-1 Nishi-Shinjuku | 2–8-1 西新宿 | Shinjuku-*

ku | 新宿区 | Subway E 28 Tochō-mae | Yamanote loop line Shinjuku

SHINJUKU GYOEN (新宿御苑) ●
(130 B–C6) (*Ⓜ F–G6*)

In 1989, the Shinto funeral ceremony for the deceased emperor Hirohito was held in the Japanese section of the garden. Following the Meiji Restoration in 1868, possession of the garden – a delightful combination of English, French and Japanese garden architecture – was transferred from the powerful feudal lord Naitō to the imperial household. The 58,000 m²/14 acre Shinjuku Imperial Gardens – which attract many visitors, particularly during cherry blossom season – have been open to the public since the end of the Second World War. The chrysanthemum show in the autumn is another special attraction for flower lovers. However, a stroll through this green oasis is very relaxing at any time of year. *Tue–Sun 9am–4pm | Admission ¥200 | 11 Naitōmachi | 11 内藤町 | Shinjuku-ku | 新宿区 | Subway M 10 Shinjuku-gyoenmae*

OTHER DISTRICTS

DAIKANYAMA (代官山)
(134 B5) (*Ⓜ F12*)

This district, known as the "Notting Hill" or "Brooklyn" of Tokyo, stretches to the south of Shibuya Station. The quiet streets invite you to take a relaxed stroll among the charming boutiques selling products by popular designers, the art galleries, and fashionable cafés and restaurants offering foreign cuisine. Anyone who can afford a flat here is earning good money.

GINZA (銀座) ●
(136 B–C 2–3) (*Ⓜ O–P 8–9*)

In the Ginza district, Tokyo presents itself as a metropolis with a Far Eastern allure. Here you can find elegant and exclusive shopping opportunities – in both long-established shops and traditional department stores, as well as in shopping palaces featuring European luxury brand names such as Bulgari, Chanel, Cartier or Armani – all very popular with the Japanese. It is also worth taking a detour into the small side streets with their restaurants and bars, cafés, boutiques and even photography and art galleries. Nowhere else in Japan are real estate prices as high as they are in Ginza.

The ★ *Hamarikyū Garden (Hamarikyu Onshi Teien)* (132 B–C4) (*Ⓜ N–O10*) *(open daily 9am–4:30pm; closed 29 Dec–1 Jan | Admission ¥300 | Subway E 19 Shiodome)* served as a summer residence for the Tokugawa shoguns and, after the Meiji Restoration, as a resort for the imperial family. The most fascinating part of the garden is a pond that is fed by sea water according to the tides. Here, three bridges shaded by wisteria lead to a small island where you can take a break at a INSIDER TIP▶ teahouse. You can order tea for approximately £4.50/$6, sit back, relax and enjoy the view of the gently winding paths, the hills that were created long ago and the ancient Japanese pines. Or you can pull out your camera and take the classic Tokyo snapshot: an image of the teahouse with the Shiodome skyscraper district in the background!

JAPAN SWORD MUSEUM
(刀剣博物館) (133 F4) (*Ⓜ S4*)

What would the samurai have been without their swords? From the Heian period (794 to 1185) to the present (there are still a few master swordsmiths in Japan), 6000 of the most beautiful examples are collected at the Sword Museum. Only about 30 masterpieces are displayed at one time. *Tue–Sun 10am–4:30 pm | Admission ¥600 | 1-12-9 Yokoami | 1–12-9 代々木 | Sumidaku-ku | 墨田区 | www. touken.or.jp/english | Subway: Ryogoku Station, JR Sobu Line*

RiSuPia science museum, the cost is ¥500). Nowhere else will you be so aware that Tokyo is a port city – a city on the ocean – than on this heaped-up "landfill", which has also paradoxically evolved into a *romantic spot* for young couples: some of them cruise in their

Teahouse in the Hamarikyu Garden with a view of the Shiodome high-rise district

ODAIBA (お台場) (139 E3) (⦿ e3)

The artificial island of Odaiba, with its futuristic buildings, museums, recreation and shopping centres is reminiscent of a giant theme park. Here, Panasonic presents state-of-the-art electronic design at the ● ⦿ *Panasonic Center (Tue–Sun 10am–6pm | 3–5–1 Ariake | www.panasonic.com/global/corporate/center/tokyo.html | Subway U 12 Ariake)*. From crystal clear displays in 4K resolution and the latest cameras to ultramodern household appliances, as well as energy-saving concepts in futuristic homes, you are invited to try them all out! And best of all, admission is free (the only exception being: if you want to visit the *Discovery Field* on the 3rd floor of the

cars; others stroll hand in hand, looking toward the water on the artificial beach. *Yurikamome Line (starting at Shimbashi)*

INSIDER TIP ▶ SHIMOKITAZAWA
(下北沢) (132 B–C1) (⦿ N–O1)

If you ask young Tokyoites where they would like to live, the answer will often be "Shimokita". That is the nickname of this charming and chaotic student-filled district in western Tokyo, known for its second-hand shops, independent theatres, bars featuring live music (jazz, rock and blues) and small concert halls. It's here in the maze of narrow alleys surrounding a railway hub just a few minutes west of Shibuya (Keio-Inokashira Line) and Shinjuku (Odakyu Line), that trends are born. People with a creative streak, the desire for an alternative lifestyle and a fondness for the old and old-fashioned find kindred spirits here; young entrepreneurs try out business ideas ranging from the curious to the creative. Every year in February, a traditional celebration and a theatre festival are held here; in July, a music festival. In contrast to the other districts, on a stroll through these pedestrian-only streets you will find many original shops and scarcely any branches of large chains. It's no wonder that the fashion magazine *Vogue* declared Shimokita one of the coolest street-style districts in the world.

YANAKA & NEZU ★
(132 B–C1) (*⑪ N–O1*)

A hint of the old, traditional Tokyo lives on in the narrow alleyways and old wooden houses in *Yanaka* (谷中). Around 1900, painters and sculptors lived here near the art academy – among them, Taikan Yokoyama and Kanzan Shimomura, the fathers of modern Japanese painting. The Spanish painter Joan Miró even bought his brushes here in the district's art supply shops. Also worth a visit is the former studio and home of the sculptor Fumio Asakura (1883–1964). The *Asakura Museum of Sculpture* (139 E2) (*⑪ e2*) (*Tue–Thu, Sat and Sun 9:30am–4:30pm | Admission ¥500 | 7–18-10 Yanaka | Subway C 15 Sendagi | Yamanote loop line Nippori*) combines architecture from the period prior to the Second World War with a traditional private home. The courtyard features a Zen water garden and the rooftop terrace offers a 360° view. The *Yanaka Cemetery*, one of the oldest in the city, is a popular place for viewing the cherry blossoms. Nowhere else in Tokyo are there so many temples, particularly along the road to Sendagi Station. The ornate *Nezu Shrine (Nezu-jinja)* (132 B1) (*⑪ N1*) (*open daily 6am–5pm | 1–28-9 Nezu | Bunkyō-ku | Subway C 14 Nezu*) in the *Nezu* (根津) district has been designated as an Important Cultural Property. Built in 1706, it was severely damaged in the Second World War and later reconstructed. In April and May, the INSIDER TIP sumptuous blooms of over 3,000 azaleas create a feast for the eyes.

SHRINES AND TEMPLES

A good rule of thumb: Shinto shrines can be recognised by their double-beamed entrance gates, called *torii*; Buddhist temples feature pagodas and swastika ornaments. Nevertheless, their decorative elements may be quite similar. The overlap between the architectural forms is as fluid as that of the religions themselves: Shintoism, the ancient religion of Japan, which has its origins in shamanism and animism, was joined by Buddhism in the 6th century. There were no religious wars; in Japan, no one is required to choose one religion over another. The Shinto gods are usually responsible for the joyful events in life, such as births and marriages. Funerals, on the other hand, are more likely to follow Buddhist rituals.

IN OTHER NEIGHBOURHOODS

EDO-TOKYO MUSEUM (江戸東京博物館) ● **(133 F4) (** *S4)*
The history of the city of Tokyo comes to life in this futuristic building. The city fathers spared no costs here – as soon as

livery trucks cart in both flopping and frozen cargo from every port in the country. At breath-taking speed, using mysterious hand gestures and in a language that only the initiated can understand, the catch is auctioned off to wholesalers at several different spots around 5am. From crabs to mackerel to gigantic tuna, several thousand tonnes of countless species of sea creatures change hands in a period of just over an hour. Around 7am, the retail dealers arrive to make their choices

Is it me? The charming and chaotic district of Shimokitazawa is very on trend.

visitors enter, they walk across a life-size replica of the famous Nijūbashi bridge. *Tue–Fri and Sun 9:30am–5pm, Sat 9:30am–7pm | Admission ¥600 | 1–4-1 Yokoami | 1–4-1 横網 | Sumida-ku | 墨田区 | www.edo-tokyo-museum.or.jp/ english/index.html | Subway E 12 Ryōgoku | Suburban railway Sobu Ryōgoku*

FISH MARKET (築地魚市場) ★ ●
(136 C3–4) (*O–P10)*
Tokyo's Fish Market is the largest in the world. The day begins here at 2am. De-

for the day. The freshly caught selection at the Fish Market covers 90 percent of the capital city's daily fish consumption. For many years now, plans have been made to relocate the *Inner Market (Mon–Sat 5am–10am, sometimes closed Wed)* along with the halls for the wholesalers, where the famous tuna auction takes place. There are new halls in Toyusu that are ready to move in. However, as of printing, the move was on hold due to ground contamination. Therefore, usual rules remain in effect: from 5am, you

For early risers: At the world's largest fish market, the day begins at 2am.

can register for the tuna auction at the *Fish Information Centre (Osakana Fukyu Center)* at *Kachidoki Gate*. In two shifts, a total of 120 visitors can then attend the auction for slightly less than half an hour. But even without an auction, the Tokyo Fish Market is a true experience! The *Outer Market (Mon–Sat 7am–3pm, sometimes partially closed Wed | www.tsukiji.or.jp/english)* will definitely remain at its original location. There are many enticing stands that, along with fish and meat also sell fruit and vegetables, dried and preserved foods as well as souvenirs such as chopsticks or bento boxes made of bamboo. Stroll through the market and sample the freshest sushi in Japan. You can find the perfect dessert at **INSIDERTIP** *Tsukiji Sanokiya (4–11-9 Tsukiji | 4–9-11 築地)*, where a mother and daughter team bake tuna-shaped dumplings filled with sweet adzuki beans and apricots or serve delicious matcha ice cream in tuna-shaped cones. *Tsukiji | 築地 | Chūo-ku | 中央区 | www.tsukiji-market.or.jp/tukiji_e.htm | Subway H 10 Tsukiji | Subway E 18 Tsukijishijo*

INSIDERTIP INOKASHIRA PARK
(井の頭公) (139 D2) (*ω d2*)
If you're looking for a few hours of relaxation, try Kichijō-ji. This western neighbourhood moves at a slower pace than the centre of Tokyo. Enjoy a leisurely stroll towards Inokashira Park as soon as you get off the train. The short path from the southern exit of the station takes you there past cosy cafés and little shops selling knick-knacks and vintage clothing. The densely growing trees make the park a green oasis; during cherry blossom season, it is a dream in white and pink. A large lake glistens in the middle of the park. Take the time to hire a rowing boat – but beware: the temple on the lake shore is dedicated to the jealous goddess Benzaiten, who is said to place curses on amorous couples! Alternatively, you can visit the small zoo *(Tue–Sun 9:30am–5pm | Admission ¥400)* in

the northern section of the park. Or follow the signs to the *Ghibli Museum* (see p. 112). *Free admission | 1 Kichijoji-Minami | 1 吉祥寺南 | Musashino City | 武蔵野市 | Suburban railway Chuo Kichijoji*

JAPAN FOLK CRAFTS MUSEUM (日本民藝館) (139 D3) (*C10*)

Mingei – arts of the people – is a term coined by museum founder Yanagi Sōetsu. During the Second World War, the institution – which opened in 1936 – barely escaped the sea of flames ignited by the firebombs. Of the more than ten thousand objects in the museum's collection – lacquered boxes and papier-mâché dolls, miniature shrines and chests of drawers, ceramics and much more – approximately one thousand are on display at a time. The museum buildings are also beautiful: the replica of a farmhouse from the Tochigi Prefecture houses the permanent collection while the offices are located in the massive farmstead gate.

Tue–Sun 10am–5pm | Admission ¥1100| 4-3-33 Komaba | 4-3-33 駒場 | Meguro-ku | 目黒区 | www.mingeikan.or.jp/ english | Inokashira railway (from Shibuya – do not take an express train!) Komaba-Todai-mae

KANDA MYÔJIN SHRINE (神田明神) (132 C4) (*O3*)

The shrine buildings, replicas constructed in 1934, are an excellent example of the Gongen architectural style of the early Edo period. The red and gold colours and numerous Buddhist motifs are reminiscent of a Chinese temple. In odd-numbered years, on one weekend in mid-May, the shrine is the site of the ● INSIDER TIP ▶ *Kanda-Matsuri*, Tokyo's second largest shrine festival, featuring processions with portable shrines and classical dance performances. *2–16-2 Soto-Kanda | 2–16-2 外神田 | Chiyoda-ku | 千代田区 | Subway M 20 Ochanomizu*

KOISHIKAWA KÔRAKUEN (小石川後楽園) (132 A3) (*M3*)

At Koishikawa Kôrakuen, Chinese and Japanese garden and landscape art flow into each other thanks to a joint effort by the third Tokugawa Shōgun, Mitsukuni and the Chinese scholar Zhu Shunshui. Tokugawa Yorifusa, the nephew and deputy of the second Shōgun, began the project in 1629; it was completed 30 years later. The path through the garden is fantastical journey to the most beautiful landscapes of China and Japan. Mount Lushan, the dam in the West Lake near Hangzhou, the hills of Arashiyama, and Hōraijima, the legendary island of immortality – all these sites and more are symbolised by the bridges, ponds, stones and lanterns. The 7000 m² (1.7 acre) garden is a true feast for the eyes. *Open daily 9am–5pm; closed 29 Dec–3 Jan | Admission ¥300 |1–6-6*

Kōraku | 1–6-6 行楽 *| Bunkyō-ku |* 文京区 *| Subway E 06, N 10 Iidabashi*

MUSEUM OF CONTEMPORARY ART TOKYO (東京都現代美術館) (139 E2–3) (*ω e2–3*)

This urban museum was designed as a centre for contemporary art. Approximately 3500 works are displayed in rotation, along with travelling exhibitions. At the time of printing, the museum was temporarily closed for renovation. *Tue–Sun 10am–6pm | Admission ¥500 | 4–1-1 Miyoshi | 4–1-1* 三 好 *| Kōtō-ku |* 江東区 *| www.mot-artmuseum.jp/eng/index.html | Subway S 12 Kikukawa | Subway T 13 Kibay*

RIKUGIEN (六義園) (139 E2) (*ω e2*)

The powerful figures of the Edo period sought rest and relaxation in this garden. Its creator, Yoshiyasu Yanagisawa, an influential feudal lord and advisor to the Shōgun Tsunayoshi Tokugawa, created replicas of 88 landscapes from Japanese and Chinese literature here. On a walk through the nearly 90,000 m²/22 acre park, you can let your imagination roam. Then the pond will become a sea, the hill a mountain and the little brook a river. At the beginning of the Meiji period, the founding family of the Mitsubishi Corporation acquired the adjoining land along with the garden; however, they donated it to the city in 1938. The garden is notable for its many birds, particularly in winter (wild ducks and herons), as well as the plum blossoms in late February and the coloured leaves in autumn. *Open daily 9am–4:30pm | Admission ¥300 | 6–16-3 Honkomagome | 6–16-3* 本駒込 *| Bunkyō-ku |* 文京区 *| Subway N 14 Komagome*

SENGAKUJI (泉岳寺) (139 E2) (*ω e2*)

Scarcely any story is so well known in Japan as that of the 47 Rōnin. It is an ever-recurring subject of puppet plays, Kabuki theatre, television dramas and films. In 1701, Lord Asano having been provoked by Lord Kira, drew his sword inside Edo Castle. It was an offence which he paid for with his life. His followers became Rōnin – samurai without a master. Forty-seven members of this loyal group decided to avenge their master's death. Almost two years later, they attacked Kira's

LOW BUDGET

For 2000 Yen, the GRUTT Pass provides free or discounted admission to 45 tourist sites (mostly museums, but also zoos). It is valid for two months as of first use and can be purchased in tourist information offices, Lawson 24-hour shops and some hotels.

The map and travel guide from the Tokyo Metropolitan Government (available at the tourist information office in City Hall) contains tear-out coupons for reduced admission at some museums. They also offer very inexpensive neighbourhood or themed tours and guided walks (also in English). *Mon–Fri (except public holidays and New Year's Day) | Start: 10am or 1pm | Reserve at least three days in advance |www.gotokyo.org*

● Free cycling tour around the Imperial Palace: Sundays from 10am, 150 bicycles are free to hire next to the Kokyomae police box **(132 B1)** (*ω N7*). Not available on rainy days or from late December to late January! *Subway C 10 Nijubashimae*

A feast for the eyes: A shady spot under a cherry tree in full bloom in Koishikawa Kōrakuen

residence, killed him and carried his severed head to Asano's tomb in triumph. Asano's honour was restored. However, like thier master, the 47 Rōnin were sentenced to death by ritual suicide.

In the Buddhist Sengakuji Temple, the master and his followers are buried side by side. In the temple grounds, the well still stands where the Rōnin washed Kira's head before presenting it to their master. The two-storey main entrance gate, built in 1836, is particularly interesting from an architectural standpoint. *April–Sept open daily 7am–6pm, Oct–March until 5pm | Free admission; Museum ¥500 | 2–11-1 Takanawa | 2–11-1 高輪 | Minato-ku | 港区 | Subway A 07 Sengakuji*

TOKYO SKYTREE (東京スカイツリー) ★ ☆ (139 E2) (*M e2*)

The Skytree, the largest free-standing radio tower in the world, extends exactly 634 m/2,080 ft into the air, making the capital city's remaining skyscrapers look like little brothers and sisters. Tickets for the building's opening were sold out weeks in advance. No wonder: the view of the entire Kanto region from 350 or 450 m/1148 or 1476 ft is second to none. In the base of the tower as well as in the adjoining buildings, there are shops, restaurants, an aquarium and much more. *Open daily 8am–10pm | Admission ¥2060 for the lower, ¥3090 for both observation decks; priority tickets for quick entry: ¥3000 or ¥4000| 1–1-13 Oshiage | 1–1-13 押上 | Sumida-ku | 墨田区 | www.tokyo-skytree.jp/en | Subway A 20, Z 14 Oshiage*

TOKYO TOWER (東京タワー) ☆ (136 A4) (*M L10*)

This replica of the Eiffel Tower, completed in 1958, is probably the most obvious example of the Japanese people's love of imitation. At 333 m/ 1093 ft, the steel structure is actually 9 m/29.5 ft

Exemplifying Japan's love of imitation: Tokyo Tower, an Eiffel Tower replica

higher than the Paris original. On the ground floor there's an aquarium and on the first floor a large souvenir shop as well as several restaurants. Nevertheless, most of the visitors crowd to the lifts that take them to the 150 m/492 ft-high observation deck. Here, they can transfer to another elevator and continue to the fully glazed observation deck located 250 m/820 ft above ground. The sea of lights after sundown is a particularly striking sight. *Open daily 9am–10pm | Admission ¥900 for the lower, ¥2800 for the Top Deck | 4–2-8 Shibakōen | 4–2-8 芝公園 | Minato-ku | 港区 | www.tokyotower.co.jp/english | Subway E 21 Akabanebashi | Subway I 06 Onarimon*

YASUKUNI SHRINE (YASUKUNI-JINJA) (靖国神社) (131 F5) (*L5*)

In 1879, when the Meiji emperor gave this building its name – "Shrine of the Peaceful Country" – he could not have known what an inglorious role Japan

would play approximately six decades later. In his mind, the empire owed its peace and societal security to all those who had died in the service of the emperor, and their souls deserved to be honoured in the Yasukuni-jinja. Only a few years before, Shintoism had been declared the state religion of Japan. The national cult, according to which the *Tennō* was elevated to the status of a god – the direct descendent of the sun goddess Amaterasu – was used by political and military leaders after the First World War for their own purposes. According to them, the Japanese had been chosen by the gods to rule the world.

Every year on 15 August, the day of Japan's surrender, a bizarre spectacle takes place: Japanese ultra-nationalists, many dressed in old uniforms, make a pilgrimage to the shrine to pray for the war dead. Some government officials even participate, even though Japan's post-war constitution stipulates a separation of reli gion and state. Since 1978, the names of those who were executed by the Allies as major war criminals have also been listed in the shrine's register of the dead – including the wartime prime minister, General Tōjō. In the neighbouring Asian countries that suffered under Japanese occupation, politicians' visits to the shrine are therefore met with great indignation. In fact, all over the world, this behaviour is seen as a sign that to this day, Japan still has not truly come to terms with the atrocities that were committed during the Second World War.

The shrine complex itself reinforces this impression. The martial-looking steel *tori*, guarded by stone dogs, appears more threatening than peaceful. A certain degree of restraint prevails at the actual shrine building; countless cherry trees that reveal their sumptuous blossoms in April, the Noh stage and the white doves – there are said to be exactly 850 of them – soothe the eyes and the

spirit. Yet only a few steps away, tanks and anti-aircraft guns are lurking – replicas of the military equipment that Nippon's army deployed to such devastating effect in the Second World War. In the adjoining military museum as well *(Yūshūkan | Open daily 9am–5pm)*, one learns nothing about the wartime horrors committed by Japan, such as the 1937 Nanking Massacre, in which Japanese troops murdered hundreds of thousands of Chinese civilians and prisoners of war, or the Bataan Death March in the Philippines in 1942. *Open daily 6am–6pm | 3–1-1 Kudankita | 3–1-1 九段下北 | Chiyoda-ku | 千代田区 | Subway S 05, Z 06, T 07 Kudanshita*

YUSHIMA SHRINE (YUSHIMA-TENJIN) (湯島天神) **(132 C3)** *(ᗩ O3)*
No shrine in Tokyo is more familiar to desperate parents than this one. During the Edo period, parents would rush here to hang up notices if their children went

GIANTS VS. SWALLOWS

Baseball is the number one sport in Japan, and the most successful team of all time comes from Tokyo: the Yomiuri Giants. Founded by the Yomiuri media corporation in 1934, they are something like the Manchester United of Nippon baseball. They split the total fan base – in Tokyo as well as in the country as a whole – into two camps: the pro-Giants and the anti-Giants. The Giants fans often have the edge. The millions invested in securing star players each season pay off time after time. Tickets for home games at the often sold-out *Tokyo Dome* **(132 A3)** *(ᗩ M3))*

(Admission ¥1000 (for standing room) – ¥6200| 1–3-61 Kōraku | Bunkyō-ku | Tel. 03 58 05 21 11 | www.tokyo-dome. co.jp/e/dome | Suburban railway Chūō- or Sobu Line Suidōbashi) are available at TD ticket booths, in 24-hour Lawson shops and through the internet. The Yakult Swallows are the number two professional team in Tokyo. You can almost always purchase tickets even just before the first pitch (usually at 6pm) at the stadium ticket booth. *Meiji Jingū Stadium* **(130 C2)** *(ᗩ H8)* *(Admission ¥1800–¥4700| 3–1 Kasumigaokamachi | Shinjukuku | Tel. 03 34 04 89 99 | Subway G 03 Gaienmae).*

missing. Today, they pray for their off-spring to pass admissions tests to institutions that will advance their careers – be they prestigious kindergartens or the elite Tōdai University. The racks on which the votive tablets hang are in danger of collapsing under the weight of all the wishes;

the Buddhist Jōdō or "pure land" school, which honours the celestial redeemer Buddha Amitabha (Japanese: Amida). Approximately 3000 novices from the 6000 *Jōdō* temples located throughout Japan prepared for ordination here. The fall of the Tokugawa brought with it the

Welcome to rural Japan: Village life at the Japan Open Air Folk House Museum

after all, Yushima-tenjin honours the god of learning. *Open daily 6am–8pm | 3–30-1 Yushima | 3–30-1 湯島 | Bunkyō-ku | 文京区 | Subway M 20 Ochanomizu*

ZŌJŌJI (増上寺) (136 A4) (𝄞 M10)

The former family temple of the Tokugawa shōguns reflects none of their former might. However, there is no other site that so clearly illustrates the influence on the city landscape of the political and societal changes that have taken place since the Meiji era. With 48 affiliated temples and approximately 150 school buildings, between 1598 and 1868, the Zōjōji was the administrative and spiritual centre of

expropriation of the temple. Still worth seeing are *Sanmon*, the "Gate of Triple Redemption" and the 15 t bronze bell, the largest in eastern Japan. On New Year's Eve, Zōjōji radiates some of its former appeal for a brief time: thousands of Tokyoites want to be present at the turn of the New Year, when the huge bronze bell is sounded exactly 108 times in the *Joya no kane*. Large throngs also gather for *Setsubun*, a festival that takes place on 3 or 4 February, celebrating the end of winter. At the call *"Oni wa soto – fuku wa uchi!"* ("Devils out, fortune in!"), people throw beans into the air to drive away everything that is evil. *Open daily 9am–*

5pm | 4–7-35 Shibakōen | 4–7-35 芝公園 | Minatoku | 港区 | Subway I 06 Onarimon

OUTSIDE THE CITY

FUJI-SAN (富士山) ★ (0) (∅ 0)

When we think of Japan, we are sure to picture the perfect beauty of the majestic Mount Fuji. Japan's sacred mountain is located approximately 120 km/75 mi outside of Tokyo. In July or August, a climb up the 3776 m/12,400 ft-high volcano is quite possible with a little preparation. You need to be fit and healthy and have two free days as well as appropriate clothing for a mountain hike (hiking boots; a warm, waterproof jacket; rain trousers; gloves and a warm cap), a torch and as a precaution, a can of oxygen (available in sports shops) for the thinner air above 3000 m/9800 ft.

The drive to the fifth mountain station takes about two and a half hours. In summer, busses run by the Keio and Fujikyu companies leave regularly from the western exit of Shinjuku Station. From the mountain station, the climb is four to six hours on foot to the summit of the dormant volcano (the last eruption was in 1776); you should plan about three hours for the descent. Some climbers spend the night in one of the mountain huts along the way. This way, if you start very early, you can be standing at the top of the sacred Fuji-san at sunrise – a once-in-a-lifetime experience!

Still, there are two things you should keep in mind: Fuji is a mountain to be taken seriously. The weather can be capricious, and even in the summertime there can be frost at the summit area. Also, it is so high that sensitive people may experience some symptoms of altitude sickness (headaches or nausea). Every season, up to half a million people scale Japan's highest peak (avoid the weekends!) – from small children to the elderly. The simplest way is to book an organised tour: for example, with the highly knowledgeable Fujiyama Guides *(www.fujiyamaguides.com/english/tours/index.html)*. Further information: *www.city.fujiyoshida.yamanashi.jp/div/english/html/index.html*

INSIDER TIP ▶ JAPAN OPEN AIR FOLK HOUSE MUSEUM (日本民家園) (139 D3) (∅ d3)

Just a 20-minute train ride and 15-minute walk, and you arrive in the rural Japan of days gone by. In this hilly park in Kawasaki, comfortable shoes are a must! Here you will find a charming arrangement of 25 traditional buildings that have been transplanted from various sections of the country along with their historic furnishings. You can also see a village Kabuki theatre with a hand-operated rotating stage, as well as a storehouse on stilts. There are regular demonstrations of handicrafts such as basket making or weaving – and you are invited to try them yourself! A traditional inn serves soba and other Japanese dishes. *Nov–Feb: Tue–Sun 9:30am–4:30pm; March–Oct 9:30am–5pm; closed on days following public holidays and 29 Dec–3 Jan | Admission ¥500; free tours in English by appointment | 7–1-1 Masugata | 7–1-1 枡形 | Tama-ku | 多摩区 | Kuwasaki City | 川崎市 | www.city.kawasaki.jp/en | Odakyū Line from Shinjuku to Mukougaoka-yūen*

KAMAKURA (鎌倉) ★ (138 C5) (∅ c5)

The train trip from Tokyo *(Shonan-Shinjuku or Yokosuka Line)* to Japan's historic capital takes just under an hour. From 1192 to 1333, Kamakura (pop. today 170,000) was the political and military centre of the country. Several dozen shrines and temples – many of them are among the most beautiful in Japan – bear witness to this glorious era. Furthermore, Kamakura features a one-km/0.6-mile-long sandy beach.

It is best to exit the train one station early, at Kita-Kamakura. To the left of the station is the Zen temple *Engakuji (open daily March–Nov 8am–4:30pm, Dec–Feb 8m–4pm | Admission ¥300)*; the *Shariden* reliquary is the oldest Zen structure in Japan. The country's oldest Zen monastery, *Kenchoji (open daily 8:30am–4:30pm | Admission ¥300)*, built in 1253, is just a 15-minute walk away. After this, the train ride to Kamakura takes only a few minutes. If you want to see its many historic sites, it is best to take local buses or INSIDER**TIP** hire a bicycle. From the station's eastern exit, take the small stairway on the right up to the *Kurarin* rental service *(open daily 8:30am–5pm | Prices start at ¥1600 per day)*. Most of Kamakura's most popular tourist sites are located to the west of the railway tracks: the *Daibutsu (Great Buddha) (open daily April–Sept, 8am–5:30pm, Oct–March 8am–5pm | Admission ¥200)*, a massive bronze

monument dating from 1252, looks down at the crowds of visitors from a height of almost 12 m/39 ft. Equally popular are the *Hase-Kannon Temple (Hasedera) (open daily March–Sept. 8am–5pm, Oct–Feb 8am–4:30pm | Admission ¥300)* with its gilded wooden statue of Kannon, the goddess of mercy – and the city's most important sacred place, the Shinto shrine *Tsurugaoka Hachimangu (open daily April–Sept 5am–8:30pm, Oct–March 6am–8:30pm | Admission to Shrine Museum ¥200)* near the station.

The crowds are quite a bit smaller at the holy sites to the east of the railway line. At the *Zuisenji Temple (open daily 9am–5pm | Admission ¥200)*, you can unwind with a walk through the beautiful garden. The INSIDER**TIP** *Jomyoji-Tempel (open daily 9am–4pm | Admission ¥100)* also offers culinary delights: on a small rise, a restaurant serves first-class cuisine in a lovely garden *(Tue–Sun 10am–5pm)*. The ● *Hokokuji-Tempel (open daily 9am–4pm | Admission ¥200)* invites you to linger at its teahouse in a bamboo grove. Relax with a green matcha tea and sweets for ¥500 and enjoy the view of a small waterfall.

FIT IN THE CITY

The circle around the Imperial Palace, just over 5 km/3 mi long, may not be Tokyo's most beautiful jogging route, but it's definitely the most popular. At weekends, amateur athletes and running groups as well as competitive university and corporate clubs meet at the Sakuradamon **(132 A–B1)** *(ω M7)*. On workdays, mostly ministry officials and employees from the nearby office towers huff and puff past the palace on

their midday breaks. Sunday mornings are the best time to jog: car traffic to the right of the running path is not as heavy then. Joggers always run anti-clockwise. Recently there have been many complaints about rude joggers, so please be considerate of pedestrians! You can find more information about jogging in Tokyo on the "Namban Rengo" website, managed by the "Barbarian horde" club: *www.namban.org*.

Brochures are available at the *Tourist Information Centre* in the railway station (eastern exit).

KAWAGOE (川越) (139 D1) (*ℳ d1*)

It is easy to see why Kawagoe is also known as Little Edo. This city, located 40 km/25 mi northwest of Tokyo, was once a flourishing trading post. Several dozen of the old trading houses are still stand-

or standing on the temple grounds are 538 stone disciples of Buddha. None of the **INSIDER TIP** *Gohyaku-Rakan Statues* is exactly like another: they are fat and thin, straight and crooked, with expressions ranging from mischievous to grave and sad. Legend has it that if you visit after dark, you will notice that one statue feels particularly warm. If you return by daylight, you will see that this is the

A textbook Buddha: Daibutsu in Kamakura

ing in all of their former glory along the *Ichibun-gai* and its side streets. Children will love the *Kashiyayokocho*, a narrow row of shops where traditional sweets are sold. Four times a day, the bell rings in the three-story wooden tower, *Tokino Kane*, which dates back to the 17th century. Be sure to visit the old *Edo Castle* that Shōgun Iemitsu had moved to Kawagoe from the capital. The sections of the castle that still remain today exude dignity and tranquillity. Also sitting, lying

figure that resembles you the most. If you happen to be here on the 28th day of the month, don't miss the popular **INSIDER TIP** *Kawagoe Antique Market* at the *Naritasan-Betsuin* temple, just a few minutes' walk to the north. Information and maps (in English and other languages) are available at the *Tourist Information Office (open daily 9am–4:30pm)* at the railway station or at *www.koedo. or.jp/foreign/english. Express train on the Tobu-Tojo Line (30 min.)*

FOOD & DRINK

Japan is indisputably a nation of gourmets. Tokyo boasts more restaurants with Michelin stars than any other city – Paris included.

Of course, some of the prices are also at the five-star level. But don't worry: in Tokyo you have a vast selection ranging from truly cheap to extremely expensive – and often for very little money, you will not only be satisfied but also amazed at how good it tastes. Ordering is not as difficult as you might imagine as many restaurants have display windows featuring plastic replicas of the dishes they offer. Menus with photographs or English descriptions are also increasingly common. For noodle lovers, the culinary starting point is easy. Choose between Chinese noodles (rāmen) and Japanese noodles

made from buckwheat (soba) or wheat flour (udon) prepared in countless different ways. The rule is: slurping is allowed and even welcome. It is said to improve the taste. For a rustic meal, you usually can't go wrong at a Yakitori, Izakaya or Robatayaki restaurant, each with a red lantern at the entrance. They vary only in the size and selection of their dishes. The smells in the surrounding area are often irresistible: meat, vegetables and sometimes fish are grilled to perfection on small wooden skewers. The most suitable beverages here are beer and rice wine (sake). An indispensable element of Japanese cuisine is vegetables, mushrooms, fish and shrimps fried in a light coating of batter – you will quickly learn to love tempura!

Sushi and beyond. It doesn't have to be raw fish – Tokyo's cuisine features a range of delicacies – such as Tempura or Teppanyaki

Equally tourist-friendly are the beef dishes sukiyaki and shabushabu – a kind of fondue – or teppanyaki: thin slices of beef or pork with vegetables cooked on a hot steel plate. All three of these dishes are prepared at the table. In some restaurants you can enjoy Kobe or Matsusaka beef – these finely marbled, melt-in-your-mouth meats are as expensive as they are famous.

Yet another specialty is eel (unagi), which is served topped with a mixture of sweet rice wine and soy sauce. Eat it in the hottest part of the summer, say the Japanese, to revive your spirits and lend you stamina. Kaiseki-ryōri is Japan's ultimate gastronomic pleasure – and it comes at a high price. This series of mini-iature menus – composed of tiny appetisers artfully arranged on colour-coordinated lacquered dishes – evolved out of the tea ceremony; it is a feast for the eyes filled with seasonal references. At least once – perhaps for a cheaper midday meal – you should indulge in this luxury in order to experience Japanese culinary culture in its aesthetic perfection and in the corresponding setting.

Fish served in its purest form is a fundamental element of Japanese cuisine. Whether it's served on balls of vinegar-seasoned rice as sushi or cut into thin slices as sashimi, raw fish can really melt in your mouth and taste divine. The best place to get it is in a sushi-ya, at

For a break from eating in restaurants, onigiri are a very popular takeaway meal. This is rice pressed into triangle or ball shapes and filled with tuna, salmon, pickled brown kelp or beef that can serve as a light lunch. Other good snacks are rice crackers (senbei), which are available in all different flavours. You can find both of these things in conveni-

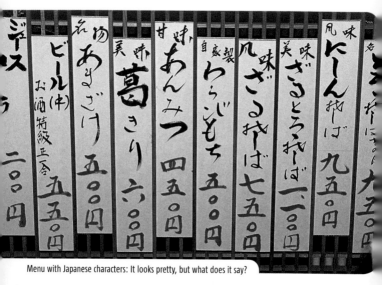

Menu with Japanese characters: It looks pretty, but what does it say?

the counter where you can order simply by pointing your finger. Alternatively, you can't go wrong by letting the sushi chef choose for you and asking for omakase – literally, the cook's recommendation.

If you want to season your culinary experience with a bit of a thrill, a fugu restaurant is the right place for you. The liver of the otherwise friendly-looking pufferfish is so poisonous that eating an improperly prepared fugu dish can have deadly consequences. Naturally, all the chefs are specially trained. Fugu season lasts from October to March.

ence stores, which are rarely more than a five minute walk from wherever you are. But please don't eat while walking down the street or sitting on the subway; this is highly frowned-upon in Japan.

A few more words about beverages: wine drinkers will only find quality products in Western luxury shops – for a hefty price. But beer or sake are better compliments to Japanese cuisine in any case. There are also refreshing long drinks with shōchū (schnapps) as a base. A slightly sweeter alternative is umeshu, plum wine on the rocks or with soda.

CAFÉS

This land of green tea is also home to a significant coffee house culture. Certain cafés here present themselves with a special, often French-influenced flair. Nearly all of them are open from the late afternoon until late in the evening.

INSIDER TIP AOYAMA FLOWER MARKET TEA HOUSE (青山フラワーマーケット ティーハウス 南青山本店) (134 C3) (*∅ G9*)

In the front it's a flower shop; in the back it is a teahouse decorated with seasonal blooms. Anyone who likes greenery will love it here. *Open daily from 11am onwards | 5–1–2 Minamiaoyama | 5–1–2 南青山 | Shibuya-ku | 渋谷区 | Subway G 02, C 03, Z 02 Omotesandō*

CERISE (セリーズ) (136 B3) (*∅ N9*)

Would you like to start your day off with a treat? Luxury breakfast in an elegant setting – with an English or Japanese buffet – starts at £16/$26. *Mon–Fri from 6:30am, Sat/Sun from 7am | 1–9–1 Higashi-Shimbashi | 1–9–1 東新橋 | Minato-ku | 港区 | Subway E 19 Shiodome*

LAUDERDALE CAFÉ (ローダーデール カフェ) (135 E4) (*∅ J10*)

At this very popular café in Roppongi Hills, you can feast on pancakes, fine soufflés or omelettes from 7am onwards. On sunny days, the terrace fills up quickly. *6–15–1 Roppongi | 6–15–1 六本木 | Minato-ku | 港区 | Subway H 04, E 23 Roppongi*

LE PAIN QUOTIDIEN (ルパンコティディアン芝公園店) (136 A4) (*∅ M10*)

Excellent European-style breads and baked goods as well as delicious salads guarantee full tables, especially at the weekends. The café and adjoining bakery also feature European décor. *3–3–1 Shibakoen | 3–3–1 芝公園 | Minato-ku | 港区 | Subway I 05 Shibakoen*

⭐ **Kushiwakamaru**
The aroma of the grilled, skewered meats will make your mouth water → p. 65

⭐ **Narisawa**
Healthy culinary delights that change with the seasons → p. 67

⭐ **Restaurant Luke**
A romantic beer garden located 200 m/650 ft above the sea of Tokyo houses → p. 70

⭐ **Ichinotani**
Vegetarian variations on the hearty hotpot: sumo cuisine prepared by experts → p. 70

⭐ **Tsunahachi**
For lunch: excellent tempura at very reasonable prices → p. 73

⭐ **Edogin**
Super-fresh fish at a sushi institution near the Fish Market → p. 69

⭐ **Tentake**
The place to go for the famous pufferfish: a fugu restaurant with tradition → p. 70

⭐ **Maisen**
Wiener schnitzel, Japanese-style → p. 72

⭐ **Kanda Yabu-soba**
Tokyo's most famous soba restaurant: noodle specialities in a classic atmosphere → p. 71

MARCO POLO HIGHLIGHTS

PURE DELI & STORE (ピュアカフェデリストラ) ⊘ (134 C3) *(⑪ G9)*

This cosy, brightly-furnished organic café serves exclusively vegan delights, accompanied by organic coffee. *Open daily 9am–11:30pm | 5–10-17 Minami-Aoyama | 5–10-17 南青山 | Minato-ku | 港区 | Subway Z 02, G 02, C 04 Omotesandō*

VIRON (ヴィロン) (134 B4) *(⑪ E10)*

The baked goods at this patisserie are among the finest available in Tokyo. Despite its steep prices, the café on the first floor is always full. A good tip from those in the know is the INSIDER TIP▶ breakfast: for around £8/$11, you can order a bread basket with a large selection of jams, un-limited coffee and two pastries of your choice – and you can also get it packed to take away. *Open daily 9am–10pm | 33–8 Udagawa-cho | 33–8 宇田川町 | Shibuya-ku | 渋谷区 | Yamanote loop line Shibuya | Subway Z 01, G 01, F 16 Shibuya*

PUBS

Izakaya is the Japanese word for cosy pubs where people meet in the evenings for a beer or sake in a relaxed atmosphere. It's common practice to order a round for everyone in the group. You can often recognise *izakaya* by their red lanterns. Some pubs, like the popular *yakitoriya*, specialise in chicken dishes.

GOURMET RESTAURANTS

Kinsui ● ⤬ (131 D2) *(⑪ J2)*

Scarcely any other traditional restaurant in Tokyo is more beautifully located. In the middle of the Chinzan-sō Garden, Kinsui exudes the stately calm that is an integral part of sophisticated Japanese culinary culture. At lunch time, the Kaiseki Menu, recommended by the chef, costs upwards of £50/$70; in the evenings it starts at £105/$140 plus service and tax. Private rooms are available to hire; reservations and appropriate attire are required. *Open daily | 2–10-8 Sekiguchi | Bunkyō-ku | Tel. 03 39 43 11 11 | www.chinzanso.com/english/restaurant.html | Subway Y 12 Edogawabashi*

Nobu Tokyo (135 F3) *(⑪ L9)*

Nobu Matsuhisa is considered one of Japan's most creative and famous chefs; he also has restaurants in New York and London. Lunch a la carte starts at around £22/$30; the chef's special *(omakase)* costs about £50/$70. In the evening, main courses start at £75/$100. *Open daily | 1F Toranomon Tower Office | 4–1-28 Toranomon | Minato-ku | Tel. 03 57 33 00 70 | www.noburestaurants.com/tokyo/experience*

Sukibayashi Jiro Ginza (136 C2) *(⑪ O8)*

Three Michelin stars ensure that this restaurant, owned by the "old master" of sushi, Jiro Ono and his son, is always full. The delicacies change according to the seasons and cost over £220/$290. But slow eaters will not be happy here: some guests report being dispatched very quickly. Japanese language skills are required. *Closed Sat, Sun, holidays and in mid-August | B1F Tsukamoto Sogyo Bldg. | 4–2-15 Ginza | Chūo-ku | Tel. 03 35 35 36 00 | www.sushi-jiro.jp/shopinfo | Subway M 16, H 08, G 09 Ginza*

Relaxed and informal: A typical pub with long wooden tables

INSIDER TIP HANTEI (はん亭)
(132 C1) (*∅ O1*)

This pub near the Ueno Park is worth a visit for its traditional wooden interior décor alone. The *kushiage*, an elegant fried version of the traditional yakitori meat skewers that originated in Ōsaka, is especially delicious. *Closed Mondays | 2–12-15 Nezu | 2–12-15 根津 | Bunkyō-ku | 文京区 | Tel. 03 38 28 14 40 | Subway C 14 Nezu | Moderate*

HOKKAIDO (北海道) (134 C6) (*∅ G12*)

Northern Japanese specialities such as prawns are served on the 39th floor of the Yebisu Garden Place. Place your order via a touchscreen. *Open daily | 4–20-3 Ebisu | 4–20-3 恵比寿 | Shibuya-ku | 渋谷区 | Tel. 03 54 48 95 21 | Subway H 02 Ebisu | Yamanote loop line Ebisu | Budget*

KUSHIWAKAMARU (串若丸) ★
(134 B6) (*∅ E12*)

Everything you expect from a yakitori pub: Spartan furnishings, but a comfortable atmosphere; always full, and all the skewered meats are simply deli-cious. The portions here are particularly generous and long queues are not unusual. *Open daily | 1–19-2 Kami-Meguro | 1–19-2 上目黒 | Meguro-ku | 目黒区 | Tel. 0337 15 92 92 | Subway H 01 Naka-meguro | Budget*

INSIDER TIP MANMAYA (まんまや慶応 仲通り店) (135 E4) (*∅ K10*)

This popular izakaya is located in a pub-lined alley near Keio University, in an old farmhouse that is easily recognised by its red paper umbrella. Guests are seated on tatami mats or at tables; small private rooms are available for groups. Excellent value for money! *Open daily | 5–20-20 Shiba | 5–20-20 芝 | Minato-ku | 港区 | Tel. 03 57 65 28 65 | Subway I 04, A 08 Mita | Yamanote loop line Tamachi | Budget*

NANBANTEI (南蛮亭) (135 E3) (*∅ K9*)

The main branch of this yakitori chain is also popular among Tokyo's foreign residents. Friendly service. *Closed Saturdays | 4–5-6 Roppongi | 4–5-6 六本木 | Minato-ku | 港区 | Tel. 03 34 02 06 06 | Subway H 04, E 23 Roppongi | Moderate*

STAND BY FARM (スタンドバイファーム) ⊕ (136 C2) (⬚ O8)

In this strictly non-smoking pub, the organic vegetables come straight from the farm. Everything here — including the meat — is prepared simply but artfully, even at lunchtime. They also have a good selection of sake! The trendy atmosphere primarily attracts young people. *Open daily | 3–12-7 Ginza | 3–12-7 銀座 | Chūō-ku | 中央区 | Tel. 050 55 90 21 96 | Subway A 11, H 09 Higashi-Ginza | Moderate*

SUISUI (粋酔) (133 D2) (⬚ Q2)

Suisui serves home style cuisine in a cheerful atmosphere. The selection of over 100 rice wines is a highlight. For a set price of approx. £26/$35 you can drink as much sake as you want and are able to in two hours. *Closed Sun and holidays | 3–35-9 Higashiueno | 3–35-9 東上野 | Taito-ku | 台東区 | Tel. 03 68 03 07 18 | Subway G 17 Inari-chō | Moderate*

TAKETOMI JIMA (竹富島) (136 C2) (⬚ O8)

Here you can find the flavours of Taketomi jima, an island in Okinawa known for its deep blue sea and fantastic beaches. Try the umibudō, a grape-like, salty-tasting sea vegetable, and the "national dish" goya champuru, a pan-cooked meal of egg, tofu, pork and bitter melon. *Open daily | Daito Ginza Bldg. B1F | 大東銀座ビル B1 | 6–12-13 Ginza | 6–12-13 銀座 | Chūō-ku | 中央区 | Tel. 03 55 37 12 93 | Subway M 16, H 06, G 09 Ginza | Budget*

TOTOSHIGURE SHIMOKITAZAWA (ととしぐれ・下北沢店) (0) (⬚ A10)

There are countless great pubs in lively Shimokitazawa, but this izakaya is exceptionally good. You can watch the nimble chefs working at the counter, which is decorated with fresh vegetables. Inside,

FOR BOOKWORMS AND FILM BUFFS

Who is Mr. Satoshi? by Jonathan Lee (2010) — A photographer goes in search of a mysterious figure in his deceased mother's life — and stumbles upon 60 years' worth of intertwining mysteries.

The Hare with Amber Eyes: A Hidden Inheritance by Edmund de Waal (2010) — A combination memoir and detective story: the author traces his family's history through an inherited collection of Japanese art.

The Scarlet Gang of Asakusa by Yasunari Kawabata — First published in 1930, this novel by a Nobel Prize-winning author captures the allure of Asakusa, once known as the "Montmartre of Tokyo".

Adrift in Tokyo (2007) — A broad, quirky comedy by Satoshi Miki, following two miserable characters on an entertaining journey through Tokyo's many districts and suburbs.

Lost in Translation (2003) — Two lonely Americans meet in Tokyo: since the release of this Oscar-winning film by Sofia Coppola, Shibuya Crossing has become the most photographed intersection in the world.

Shall We Dance? (1997) — In Masayuki Suo's original film, a successful but lonely salaryman discovers his secret passion. A 2004 Hollywood remake starred Richard Gere and Jennifer Lopez.

you sit at low tables with foot space underneath; outside seating is on a narrow wooden terrace. From the southern exit of the train station, follow the sloping street straight down and you'll be there in just over five minutes. *Open daily | 5–30-12 Daizawa | 5–30-12 代沢 | Setagaya-ku | 世田谷区 | Tel. 050 73 02 06 18 | totoshigureshimokitazawa. com | Suburban railway Odakyu, Keio Inokashira Shimokitazawa | Budget*

RESTAURANTS: EXPENSIVE

TEMPURA HATANAKA (天ぷら畑中)
(135 E4) (*𝄞 K11*)

This small tempura restaurant is known for its unusual and top-quality ingredients. For his crispy tempura dishes, which have been awarded a Michelin star, Chef Hiroyoshi Hatanaka uses oysters or flower blossoms, depending on the season. He can advise you in English on your selection of deep-fried delicacies. *Open daily | 2–21-10 Azabujuban | 2–21-10 麻布十番 | Minato-ku | 港区 | Tel. 03 34 56 24 06 | Subway N 04, E 22 Azabujuban*

KITAOHJI SHINJUKU SARYO (北大路 新宿茶寮) ♨ (130 A5) (*𝄞 E5*)

Here you can enjoy Kaiseki menus on the 51st floor. Private seating is available for groups (seated on the floor with foot space under the table); the waitresses wear kimonos. *Closed Sun, holidays | 2–6-1 Nishishinjuku | 2–6-1 西新宿 | Shinjuku-ku | 新宿区 | Tel. 03 59 09 72 27 | Subway E 28 Tochōmae*

NARISAWA (ナリサワ) ★ ❀
(135 D2) (*𝄞 H8*)

With his French-inspired menus that vary with the seasons, Yoshihiro Narisawa combines his award-winning culinary artistry with his passion as an environ-

Hand-picked: Star cook Yoshihiro Narisawa in his restaurant

mentalist and nature lover. All of the ingredients come from hand-picked farms that use no chemical agents. Even people with allergies or lactose intolerance can dine worry-free in this minimalistic ambience as the restaurant serves specially modified dishes. Be sure to make reservations! *Open daily | 2–6-15 Minami Aoyama | 2–6-15 南青山 | Minato-ku | 港区 | Tel. 03 57 85 07 99 | Subway E 24, Z 03, G 04 Aoyama-Itchome*

SERYNA HONTEN (瀬里奈)
(135 E3) (*𝄞 K9*)

Sample the famous Kobe beef – and of

LOCAL SPECIALITIES

Ba-sashi – Horse meat sashimi

Chanko-nabe – A hearty meat and vegetable hotpot, the favourite dish of sumo wrestlers

Chirashi-zushi – Strips of shellfish, vegetables and omelette atop a bowl of vinegar-seasoned rice

Chūtoro, Ōtoro – The fattiest parts of a tuna's belly; the *non plus ultra* for connoisseurs

Ginnan – Skewered gingko nuts; a good accompaniment to beer or sake

Hiya-yakko – Cold tofu with soy sauce, herbs and bonito flakes

Mochi – A chewy sweet made of mashed rice (Photo right)

Oden – Soup with added ingredients: vegetables, hard-boiled eggs, tofu, etc. – very popular in winter

Okonomi-yaki – A type of omelette made from meat, vegetables, shrimp and squid, also known as "Monja-yaki" in Tokyo

Tempura-soba, Tempura-udon – Soup with buckwheat or wheat noodles (photo left), sometimes topped with deep-fried prawns

Tonkatsu – Pork chop with a hearty sauce

Tsukune – Skewered chicken meatballs

Una-don – Charcoal-grilled eel filets with a thick sauce made of soy and sweet sake, served over rice

Yakiimo – Baked sweet potatoes. If you hear someone call out *"oishiiimoo"*: get there as fast as you can! The potatoes taste best fresh from the mobile carts.

Zaru-soba – Cold soba noodles. Dip them in a sauce flavoured with soy, horseradish and sliced spring onions.

course, "normal" beef as well – in a dignified atmosphere. The meat may be cooked on hot stones *(ishiyaki)*, as *shabushabu* (a fondue of thinly sliced beef) or *sukiyaki*-style in a hearty, slightly sweet broth served with egg. *Open daily | 3–12-2 Roppongi | 3–12-2 六本木 | Minato-ku | 港区 | Tel. 03 34 02 10 51 | Subway H 04, E 23 Roppongi*

INSIDER TIP ▶ **TŌFUYA UKAI** (とうふ屋 うかい) (136 A4) (*ᗰ L10*)

A very special culinary experience. The heart of this locale is a finely furbished, 200-year-old sake brewery complete with a warehouse. Here, guests are greeted by friendly ladies in kimonos. The brewery is surrounded by a beautiful garden, decorated with lanterns and carp ponds. Tofu is the main ingredient in the delicious dishes. Reservations recommended. *Open daily | 4–4-13 Shiba-koen | 4–4-13 芝公園 | Minato-ku | 港区 | Tel. 03 34 36 10 28 | Subway E 21 Akabanebashi*

RESTAURANTS: MODERATE

A 16 (エーシックスティーン) (136 B1) (⁄⁄⁄ O7)

If your taste buds are craving something other than Japanese food for a change,

wooden veranda is full at lunchtime even on chilly days, thanks to the outdoor heating unit. *Open daily | 2–2-5 Azabujūban | 2–2-5 麻布十番 | Minato-ku | 港区 | Tel. 03 37 98 31 91 | Subway O4, E 22 Azabujūban*

EDOGIN (江戸銀) ★ (136 C3) (⁄⁄⁄ O9)

Only a little rice, but plenty of fresh fish: this sushi institution located near the Fish Market has based its reputation on this simple formula. If you're feeling adventurous and have plenty of money in

Intimate dining with a view of the Japanese garden: One of 55 tatami rooms in Tōfuya Ukai

why not try a stone-oven pizza or good Italian pasta. A 16 has pleasant seating both indoors and in the green courtyard. *Open daily | Marunouchi Park Bldg. | 2–6-1 Marunouchi | 2–6-1 丸の内 | Chiyoda-ku | 千代田区 | Tel. 03 32 12 52 15 | Subway M 17 Tokyo*

EAT MORE GREENS (イートモアグリーンズ) ☺ (135 E4) (⁄⁄⁄ K11)

The name says it all – you won't find any meat at this restaurant. The vegetarian and vegan dishes made with organic ingredients and the delicious, freshly squeezed juices attract many guests to this cosy corner café every day. The

your pocket, inquire about the day's special. *Open daily | 4–5-1 Tsukiji | 4–5-1 築地 | Chūō-ku | 中央区 | Tel. 03 35 43 44 01 | Subway H 10 Tsukiji*

GONPACHI (権八) (135 D4) (⁄⁄⁄ J10)

This gigantic *kura* (storehouse or treasure house) has a rather rustic, traditional feel – both in its food and in its atmosphere. It gets very full here – not only on the weekends. Be sure to make reservations! *Open daily | 1–13-11 Nishi-Azabu | 1–13-11 西麻布 | Minato-ku | 港区 | Tel. 03 57 71 01 70 | Subway H 04, E 23 Roppongi*

ICHINOTANI (一の谷) ★
(132 C4) (*Ø P3*)

Chanko-nabe, an exquisite hotpot, is considered the favourite dish of sumo wrestlers. Ichinotani's proprietor once fought in the ring himself; nevertheless, he specialises in a vegetarian version of

A meal for the fearless: Fugu at Tentake restaurant

this hearty stew. He also knows something about antiques, as attested to by the many beautiful collector's items you can see here. Be sure to make reservations! *Closed Sun and holidays | 2–13-4 Soto-Kanda | 2–13-4 外神田 | Chiyoda-ku | 千代田区 | Tel. 03 32 51 85 00 | Subway G 14 Suehirochō*

MANDALA (マンダラ) (132 B4) (*Ø N5*)

For curry lovers: this restaurant serves above-average Indian cuisine. *Open daily | 2–17 Kanda Jinbōchō | 2–17 神田神保町 | Chiyoda-ku | 千代田 区 | Tel. 03 32 65 04 98 | westindia-group.com/mandala | Subway S 06, I 10, Z 07 Jinbōchō*

RESTAURANT LUKE (レストランルーク) ★ ☆ (137 D3) (*Ø E10*)

Located 200 m/650 ft above Tokyo's sea of houses, Luke is an exquisite French restaurant that also boasts the city's highest open-air beer garden (March–Sept). It's the perfect place for a romantic dinner and also prepares special dishes for people with allergies. Reservations required! *Open daily | 8–1 Akashichō | 8–1 明石町 | Chūōku | 中央区 | Tel. 03 32 48 02 11 | www.restaurant-luke.com/restaurant.html | Subway H 10 Tsukiji*

SHABUSHABU ONYASAI YAESU-TEN (しゃぶしゃぶ温野菜 八重洲店) (136 C1) (*Ø O7*)

When you order a *shabushabu* fondue broth – starting at £22/$30 per person – you can order as much meat, vegetables and side dishes as you can manage in 90 minutes. Choose from ten types of broth that change with the seasons. **INSIDER TIP** Ask for *surigoma* (ground sesame seeds) for your dip. Many locations throughout Japan; English menu is available on the website. *Open daily | Yaesu YK building 4F | 八重洲YKビル4F | 1–7-10 Yaesu | 1–7-10 八重洲 | Chūō-ku | 中央区 | Tel. 03 35 16 25 29 | www.onyasai.com | Subway M 17 Tokyo | Yamanote loop line Tokyo*

TENTAKE (てんたけ) ★
(136 C3) (*Ø P9*)

This traditional fugu restaurant near the Fish Market is great value for money. A further plus is the English-language menu. *Closed Sun | 6–16-6 Tsukiji | 6–16-6 築地 | Chūō-ku | 中央区 | Tel. 03 35 41 38 81 | Subway H 10 Tsukiji*

TEPPANYAKI TEN GINZA 6-CHOME (鉄板焼 天 銀座6丁目店)

(136 C3) (*ⓜ O9*)

Teppanyaki is a style of cooking meat, shellfish or vegetables on a hot plate. Be sure to get seats at the counter: the chefs put on an impressive show with their speed and agility. You can get good set menus starting at about £45/$60. Very friendly service in a lively atmosphere. *Open daily |6–14-5 Ginza | 6–14-5 銀座 | Chūō-ku | 中央区 | Tel. 03 32 48 66 69 | www.teppanyaki-ten.com/ginza6/tenginza6.html | Subway A 11, H 09 Higashi-Ginza*

TOKORI (UENO BAMBOO GARDEN) (土go里上野バンブーガーデン店)

(133 D2) (*ⓜ P2*)

Here, the Korean-style *yakiniku* – meat cooked on a grill at the table – is particularly delicious. The restaurant's specialty is beef tongue and there's another special treat for train spotters – some tables have a view of Ueno Station. *Open daily | 1–52 Ueno-kōen | 1–52 上野公園 |Taito-ku | 台東区 | Tel. 03 58 07 22 55 | www.to-ko-ri.jp/shop | Subway G 16, H 17 Ueno | Yamanote loop line Ueno*

RESTAURANTS: BUDGET

INSIDERTIP ➤ CRAYON HOUSE (クレヨンハウス) ⊛ (134 C3) (*ⓜ G9*)

This vegetarian basement restaurant uses exclusively organic ingredients. Considering the quality, the lunch buffet is surprisingly inexpensive – however, the crowds are correspondingly large. Therefore, it's best to arrive before noon or after 1:30pm. In the summer there's pleasant outdoor seating. On the three floors above the restaurant, you can also find natural cosmetics, health guidebooks and wooden toys. *Open daily | 3–8-15 Kita-Aoyama | 3–8-15 北青山 | Minato-ku | 港区 | Tel. 03 34 06 64 09 | Subway G 02, Z 02, C 04 Omotesandō*

DASHICHAZUKE EN (だし茶漬けえん)

(135 E4) (*ⓜ J10*)

Ochazuke is light and delicious: a broth of green tea is poured over vegetables, fish or seaweed on a bed of rice. Several restaurant locations, including Narita Airport. *Open daily | Roppongi Hills North Tower B1F | 6–2-31 Roppongi | 6–2-31 六本木 | Minato-ku | 港区 | Tel. 03 57 72 92 96 | Subway H 04, E 23 Roppongi*

HARAJUKUGYOZARO (原宿餃子楼)

(134 B3) (*ⓜ F9*)

This is the way fried *gyoza* (filled dumplings) should be: crispy on the outside, juicy on the inside – and all at a very affordable price. It's no wonder that the queues here can be very long. By the way, the boiled version is just as delicious. *Open daily | 6–2-4 Jingumae | 6–2-4 神宮前 | Shibuya-ku | 渋谷区 | Tel. 03 34 06 47 43 | Yamanote loop line Harajuku*

ICHIOKU (一億) (135 E3) (*ⓜ K9*)

Is it Japanese cooking with a Western influence, or Western cuisine with a Japanese flair? Try it out for yourself! In any case, both natives and foreigners love this tiny, cosy restaurant, where even the toilets have a distinctive character. *Open daily | 4–4-5 Roppongi | 4–4-5 六本木 | Minato-ku | 港区 | Tel. 03 34 05 98 91 | Subway H 04, E 23 Roppongi*

KANDA YABU-SOBA (やぶそば) ★

(132 C4) (*ⓜ O4*)

Tokyo's most famous soba restaurant has been pleasing fans of buckwheat noodle soup for over 135 years. In 2014, it relocated to new premises after a fire. Be sure to try the seasonal specialities such as soba with oysters and wakame in the winter. Cash only. *Closed Wed | 2–10 Kanda-Awajichō |*

LOW BUDGET

Between 11:30am and 2pm, you can eat very cheaply. Even expensive establishments offer special lunch menus.

Teishoku are reasonably priced trays starting at about £5/$7.50, including fish, meat or tempura as well as miso soup, rice, pickled vegetables, sometimes a small dessert, and green tea. For example, at *Kōjikura* **(134 B2)** *(Ⓜ N8) (open daily at lunchtime) | Chiyoda Bldg. B1 and B2 | 1–6–4 Yūrakuchō | Chiyoda-ku | Tel. 0355 10 55 77 | Subway C 09, H 07 Hibiya | Yamanote loop line Yūrakuchō).*

Tachigui means "to eat standing up". Stand-up snack bars at large railway stations, such as Shinjuku (south entrance, Minami-guchi, behind the barrier, left) offer very inexpensive noodle dishes: soba, udon or ramen start at about £2.50/$3.50.

If you aren't feeling ravenous, you can simply visit the food section in a large department store, for example, *Isetan* **(130 B5)** *(Ⓜ F5) (3–14-1 Shinjuku | Shinjuku-ku | Subway M 09 Shinjuku-sanchōme).* There you can try some delicious free samples.

淡路町 *2–10 | Chiyoda-ku |* 千代田区 *| Tel. 03 32 51 02 87 | Subway M 19 Awajichō*

KOMAGATA DOZEU (駒方どぜう)
(133 F3) *(Ⓜ S3)*

This is the right address for adventurous gourmets. Dojō (pond loach) is a tiny, eel-like fish that is served as a stew, baked with egg, or in miso soup. It's a sepciality that the Japanese will also stand in line for before they sit down on the ground to eat it – in this traditional 19th century restaurant, guests dine seated on cushions on the floor. *Open daily | 1–7-12 Komagata | 1–7-12* 駒方 *| Taitō-ku |* 台東区 *| Tel. 03 38 42 40 01 | Subway G 19, A 18 Asakusa*

MAISEN (まい泉) ★
(134 C3) *(Ⓜ G9)*

Tonkatsu is the Japanese version of Wiener schnitzel except here it's made from pork. If you order kurobuta you will be served what is said to be the best pork in the world. *Open daily | 4–8-5 Jingūmae | 4–8-5* 神宮前 *| Shibuya-ku |* 渋谷区 *| Tel. 03 34 70 00 71 | Subway C 04, G 02, Z 02 Omotesandō*

N_1155
(エヌイレブンフィフティファイブ)
Ⓦ **(134 A6)** *(Ⓜ E12)*

Organic cuisine and no smoking allowed mean that the tapas in this Mediterranean restaurant taste twice as good. The first floor serves multi-course meals, which you can combine with carefully selected organic wines. *Closed Mon |1–1-55 Naka-Meguro | 1–1-55* 中目黒 *| Meguro-ku |* 目黒区 *| Tel. 03 37 60 10 01 | Subway H 1 Naka-Meguro*

NODAIWA (野田岩) **(135 F4)** *(Ⓜ L11)*
Serving the most delicate eel, this restaurant has known how to please its

Food hall at the Isetan department store: Here you can try all the free samples.

guests since the Edo periodw. *Closed Sun | 1–5-4 Higashi-Azabu | 1–5-4 東麻布 | Minato-ku | 港区 | Tel. 03 35 83 78 52 | Subway H 02 Akabanebashi*

INSIDER TIP ▶ SORANOIRO (ソラノイロ)
(131 F6) (*L6*)

Nowhere does ramen noodle soup taste better than in this inconspicuous locale. No wonder that the Guide Michelin presented it with its *"Bib Gourmand"* seal of approval. The best is that unlike "normal" ramen, these noodles are also suitable for people on gluten-free, vegetarian or vegan diets. Place your orders at a ticket machine. *Closed Sat | 1–3-10 Hirakawacho | 1–3-10 平河町 | Chiyoda-ku | 千代田区 | Tel. 03 32 63 54 60 | Subway Y 15 Kōjimachi*

TAKENO SHOKUDO (たけの食堂)
(136 C3) (*P9*)

The menu here revolves around sushi, sashimi and tempura. This restaurant is tucked away in a small alley near the Tsukiji-6-chome intersection. The generous portions and first-class quality especially attract Fish Market employees – and the prices are ridiculously low. Arrive before 6pm. *Closed Sun and holidays | 6–21-2 Tsukiji | 6–21-2 築地 | Chuoku | 中央区 | Tel. 03 35 41 86 98 | Subway E 18 Tsukijishijō*

TSUNAHACHI (つな八) ★

There are several Tsunahachi locations in Tokyo. What they all have in common is their pleasant, relaxed atmosphere and first-rate but inexpensive tempura selection. *Matsuya Dept. Store, 8 F | 3–6-1 Ginza | 3–6-1 銀座 (136 C2) (O8) (Open daily | Chūo-ku | 中央区 | Tel. 03 35 67 13 74 | Subway G 09, M 16 Ginza); 3–31-8 Shinjuku | 3–31-8 新宿 (130 B5) (F5) (Open daily | Shinjuku-ku | 新宿区 | Tel. 03 33 52 10 12 | Subway M 08 Shinjuku | Yamanote loop line Shinjuku)*

SHOPPING

Shopping in Tokyo, one of the world's most expensive cities? Why not! Provided, of course, you research what the desired object would cost back home.

The days are gone when you could buy Nikons, Sonys or Hitachis at rock-bottom prices in their country of origin. But if you shop tax-free, you can still find good offers – and you can often find items here that will not reach a wider market until months later.

Fashion *made in Japan* is understandably cheaper here than elsewhere – particularly in January/February and June/July, when shops make room for the latest collections. Japanese arts and crafts – from small handmade paper address books to samurai swords – are also less expensive. But even if you don't want to

Whether it's traditional design, trendy fashion or high tech; Tokyo is a consumer paradise where the danger of a spending spree is high.

buy anything, you should still take time to stroll through Tokyo's countless shopping locations. After all, they're part of Japanese culture.

Many small family businesses are open well into the evenings; the American-influenced *convenience stores* are even open round the clock. The seemingly endless underground labyrinths at the larger railway stations offer a special kind of shopping experience. In addition to the traditional department stores, *fashion buildings*, which emphasise stylish

clothing, are a magnet for shoppers. In short: nothing in Tokyo is easier than succumbing to a shopping frenzy.

But the joy of shopping in Tokyo also has many facets. The shopping street *Ameyoko* (133 D2–3) (*M P2*) is still slightly reminiscent of the end of the Second World War, when the black market flourished in this area. *Jimbocho* (132 B4–5) (*M N4–5*), where the streets are lined with antique shops, both large and small, has a significantly quieter feel. If you can, fit in a visit to Kitchen Town

ANTIQUES

or **INSIDER TIP** *Kappabashi* (133 E1–2) *(ᗰ R1–2)*. The treasures here are not just reserved for restaurant chefs. You'll find cups, plates, pots, pans, all kinds of beautiful ceramics and plastic models of sushi and other delicacies – which make an amusing souvenir! There are also extremely sharp knives, which you can have engraved with your name on the spot and everything is very reasonably priced. Strolling through the pricey *Aoyama district* (134 C3) *(ᗰ G9)*, you won't be able to decide what is most astonishing: the architecture of the luxury boutiques – from gaudy to futuristic – or their expensive window displays and subtle price tags.

clothing, coffee from sustainable farms and organic Italian specialties alongside galleries and a music bar. In the bright, open, green complex, you can dine and shop with a good conscience.

ANTIQUES

Antique shops crowd the *Kottō-dōri* (134 C3–4) *(ᗰ G10)* in Aoyama. On the Zenpukuji River to the north of Nishi-Ogikubo Station (139 D2) *(ᗰ d2)*, approximately 55 antique, second-hand and recycling shops sell everything from Japanese ceramics to American kitsch from

The latest gadgets? You'll find them in the high-tech Akihabara district

If you come to Tokyo looking for the latest in high-tech, ★ ● *Akihabara* (133 C–D4) *(ᗰ P–Q4)(www.akiba.or.jp/english)* is the right place to go. This district, with its hundreds of discount shops, is a Mecca for electronics freaks as well as manga and anime fans.

The successful music producer Takeshi Kobayashi has created a completely new shopping experience for Tokyoites: ◉ **INSIDER TIP** *Yoyogi Village* (134 B1) *(ᗰ F7)* is a green oasis with eco-friendly standards. You can find organic cotton

the 1950s. Ask for an *antikku mappu* (map) at the *kōban* (police station). At the addresses below, you can be sure to receive advice in English.

ANTIQUES NISHIKAWA (古美術 西川) (134 E4) *(ᗰ K11)*

This shop specialises in *Ko-Imari* – fine porcelain. These beautifully painted plates and cups enchanted European buyers as early as the 18th century. *Wed–Mon 11am–7pm | 2–20-14 Azabu-juban | 2–20-14 麻布十番 | Minato-ku | 港区 | Subway N 04, E 22 Azabu-juban*

ORIENTAL BAZAAR (オリエンタル バザー) ★ (134 B3) (𝄞 *F9*)

In addition to genuine antiques (and beautiful reproductions from Korea and China), you can find kimonos, woodcuts and handicrafts at reasonable prices here. *Fri–Wed 10am–7pm | 5–9-13 Jingūmae | 5–9-13 神宮前 | Shibuya-ku | 渋谷区 | www.orientalbazaar.co.jp/en/index.html | Subway G 02, C 04, Z 02 Omotesandō*

THE TOLMAN COLLECTION (ザ トルーマン コレクション) (136 B4) (𝄞 *M11*)

This gallery sells traditional and contemporary prints. *Wed–Sun 11am–7pm | 2–2-18 Shiba Daimon | 2–2–18 芝大門 | Minato-ku | 港区 | Subway E 20 Daimon*

BOOKSHOP

KINOKUNIYA (紀伊國屋) ★ (130 B6) (𝄞 *F6*)

A Mecca for bookworms. On the sixth floor you can find foreign-language books including British and American literature

– including children's books. *Open daily 10am–9pm | Takashimaya Times Square | 5–24-2 Sendagaya | 5–24-2 千駄 ヶ谷 | Shibuya-ku | 渋谷区 | Subway M 08 Shinjuku | Yamanote loop line Shinjuku*

ELECTRIC & ELECTRONIC DEVICES

LAOX DUTY FREE AKIHABARA (ラオックス DUTY FREE AKIHABARA) (133 C4) (𝄞 *P4*)

This is where you can find the largest selection of tax-free products. Other shops include the Laox Main Store, Laox Sound Shop, the stores Laox Computerkan I and II as well as the Laox Musical Instrument Shop. *Open daily 10am–7pm | 1–2-9 Soto-Kanda | 1–2-9 外神田 | Chiyoda-ku | 千代 田区 | Suburban railway Sobu Akihabara | Subway H 15 Akihabara*

YODOBASHI CAMERA (ヨドバシ カメラ) ★ (130 A5) (𝄞 *E5*)

The world's largest camera shop, with its headquarters in Shinjuku. You can find

MARCO POLO HIGHLIGHTS

Everything is so colourful here: At flea markets, you can find little treasures like these dolls.

everything here – including all the latest products. Older models may be less expensive abroad. Yodobashi also carries household appliances, mobile phones and computers. *Open daily 9:30am–10pm | 1–11-1 Nishi-Shinjuku | 1–11-1 西新宿 | Shinjuku-ku | 新宿区 | Subway M 08 Shinjuku | Yamanote loop line Shinjuku*

FLEA MARKETS

The *Tourist Information Center (TIC)* can provide current information about dates and times *(Tel. 03 32 01 33 31).*

HANAZONO SHRINE
(花園神社) ★
(130 B5) (*M F5*)
You can spend hours here, wandering between the colourful stands and looking for little treasures – and also meeting plenty of locals. *Sun approx. 8am–4pm (not on rainy days!) | 5–17-3 Shinjuku | 5–17-3 新宿 | Shinjuku-ku | 新宿区 | Subway M 09 Shinjuku-sanchōme*

OEDO ANTIQUE MARKET
(大江戸骨董市)
(136 C1) (*M O7*)
One of the largest outdoor flea markets in Japan is located in front of the Tokyo International Forum. *1st and 3rd Sun of the month 9am–4pm | 3–5-1 Marunouchi | 3–5-1 丸の内 | Chiyoda-ku | 千代田区 | www.antique-market.jp/eng/index.shtml | Yamanote loop line Yūrakuchō | Subway Y 18 Yūrakuchō | Subway C 09, H 07 Yūrakuchō Hibiya*

YASUKUNI SHRINE
(靖国神社)
(131 F5) (*M L5*)
Quite a bit smaller than the market at the Hanazono Shrine, but you can also take the time to visit the shrine itself and then take a leisurely walk over to the Imperial Palace. *Sun approx. 8am–3:30pm (no market during cherry blossom season!) | 3–1-1 Kudankita | 3–1-1 九段北 | Chiyoda-ku | 千代田区 | Subway S 05, Z 06, T 07 Kudanshita*

GALLERIES

INSIDER TIP DESIGN FESTA GALLERY (デザインフェスタギャラリー) (134 C2) (*🏠 F8*)

This location offers a forum for young creative artists to present their work. After visiting the gallery, you can relax in the little garden. *Open daily 10am–7pm | 3–20–18 Jingūmae | 3–20–18 神宮前 | Shibuya-ku | 渋谷区 | www.designfesta.com/en/about/gallery | Subway C 03, F 15 Meiji-jingūmae*

SPIRAL (スパイラル)
(134 C3) (*🏠 G9*)

In this architecturally interesting building, a stairway leads in large spirals from the ground-floor restaurant to the exhibition rooms, where art, film, fashion and music are on display. *Open daily 11am–8pm | 5–6–23 Minami-Aoyama | 5–6–23 南青山 | Minato-ku | 港区 | Subway Z 02, G 02 Omotesandō*

TOKYO PHOTOGRAPHIC ART MUSEUM (東京都写真美術館)
(134 C6) (*🏠 G12*)

Renovated in 2016, this space is a must-see for all photography lovers. Follow your visit with a walk through the Yebisu Garden Complex with its many cafés and restaurants. *Mon–Fri 10am–6pm | Price of admission varies | Yebisu Garden Place | 1–13–3 Mita | 1–13–3 三田 | Meguro-ku | 目黒区 | topmuseum.jp/e/contents/index.html | Subway H 02 Ebisu | Yamanote loop line Ebisu*

DEPARTMENT STORES

Japanese *depātos* are exquisite temples of consumption. Even the packaging from these houses has prestige value. At the beginning of each business day, all of the employees form a line, call out a cheerful "Irasshaimase! – Welcome!", and bow to you at a precise angle. The only thing missing is the red carpet. Except for a few days of the year, department stores are open between 10 or 11am and 7:30 or 9pm. If your purchases at the same store on the same day amount to more than ¥10,000 plus VAT (with the exception of food or similar products), the tax can be refunded to you the same day. Take your passport with you!

COREDO MURAMACHI (コレド室町) ★ (133 D6) (*🏠 P6*)

If your travelling companion isn't in the mood for another shopping trip, then

LOW BUDGET

The 100-yen shops *(Hyaku En Shoppu)* are great for all kinds of everyday items, and a bargain El Dorado for tourists – not just for quirky souvenir items. *Daiso* **(134 B2)** (*🏠 F8*) *(Open daily 10am–9pm | Village 107 Bldg. | 1–19–24 Jingūmae | Shibuya-ku (Takeshita-dori) | Subway C 03 Meiji-Jingūmae | Yamanote loop line Harajuku); Can-do* **(130 B4)** (*🏠 F4*) *(Open daily 11am–10pm | Seibu-Shinjuku Pepe 8F | 1–30-1 Kabukichō | Shinjuku-ku | Subway S 01, E 27 Shinjuku | Yamanote loop line Shinjuku)*

Clearance sales of luxury kimonos always take place in early January and in July/ August at the *Takashimaya* department store **(130 B4)** (*🏠 P7*) *(2–4-1 Nihombashi | Chūō-ku | Subway G 11, T 10, A 13 Nihombashi).* A third date is variable – ask someone to inquire in Japanese about the exact times *(Tel. 03 32 11 41 11).*

take them to this department store in the posh Nihombashi district. It's bound to impress even the most die-hard shopping haters. Visit the pretty Edo period-inspired shopping street between two sections of the building with its handicrafts and local delicatessens. *6–10-1 Ginza | 6–10-1 銀座 | Chūō-ku | 中央区 | Subway T 10 Nihombashi*

ISETAN (伊勢丹) (130 B5) (*⌕ F5*)

This store carries Japanese fashion by up-and-coming designers at affordable prices. The small but lovely Japanese handicraft department is also worth a visit. *3–14-1 Shinjuku |3–14-1 新宿 | Shinjuku-ku | 新宿区 | Subway M 09 Shinjuku-sanchōme*

MARUI (丸井) (130 B5) (*⌕ F5*)

In three buildings – one dedicated exclusively to men's fashion – you can find everything that is currently on trend, as well as fun accessories and attractive household items. Clearance sales in February and July offer great bargains. *3–30-13 Shinjuku | 3–30-13 新宿 | Shinjuku-ku | 新宿区 | Subway M 09 Shinjuku-sanchōme*

MITSUKOSHI (三越)
(132–133 C–D6) (*⌕ P6*)

Founded in 1673, Mitsukoshi is the flag-ship among the Tokyo department stores – it's popular with older customers. The kimono department is a sight to behold and the INSIDER TIP welcoming ceremony at the main branch at 10:30am is also spectacular. *1–4-1 Nihombashi Muromachi | 1–4-1 丸の内 | Chūō-ku | 中央区 | Subway Z 09, G 12 Mitsukoshimae*

TAKASHIMAYA (高島屋)
(137 D1) (*⌕ P7*)

Founded in the late Edo era, this department store, with its large selection of kimonos and exquisite antiques, is also committed to tradition. *2–4-1 Nihombashi | 2–4-1 日本橋 | Chūō-ku | 中央区 | Subway G 11, T 10, A 13 Nihombashi*

TAKASHIMAYA TIMES SQUARE (タカシマヤ タイムズ スクエア)
(130 B6) (*⌕ F6*)

The newest branch of the traditional department store chain consists of two building complexes joined by covered bridges. On the 12th to 14th floors, you can find a wide range of very good restaurants serving dishes from all over the world – some with access to the roof garden. A special treat for the eyes and the tastebuds is the *Food Hall* – from delicate Japanese appetisers to hearty European specialities, you can find every-

BUSINESS CARDS

In Japan, a person only becomes a true member of society once they have their own business card. After all, it answers the crucial questions at a glance: Where does this person work? What position do they hold? Are they above or below me? Strict rules of etiquette apply to all social interactions and word choices and forms of address must comply with these. For a short visit to Tokyo as a tourist, you do not need to worry about such conventions. The situation is different for business trips however; then, business cards printed in Japanese on the reverse side are a must!

thing here. *5–24-2 Sendagaya | 5–24-2 千駄ヶ谷 | Shibuya-ku | 渋谷区 | Yamanote loop line Shinjuku | Subway M 08, E 01 Shinjuku*

KIMONOS

A new silk kimono costs at least £3,000/$4,100 – plus the price of a sash *(obi)*, undergarments, etc. With a little luck, you can purchase second-hand kimonos starting at around £35/$45. Less expensive still are cotton kimonos *(yukata)*, suitable primarily as lightweight bathrobes.

CHICAGO (シカゴ) (134 B3) (*F9*)

This second-hand, young-fashion shop also carries a INSIDER TIP large selection of inexpensive kimonos and yukatas. *Open daily 11am–8pm | Olympia Annex Bldg., B1 | 6–31-21 Jingūmae | 6–31-21 神宮前 | Shibuya-ku | 渋谷区 | Subway C 03 Meijijingūmae*

HANDICRAFTS & INTERIOR DÉCOR

INSIDER TIP 2K540 AKI-OKA ARTISAN (2K540店) (133 D3) (*P3*)

This strangely named artists' colony is located directly under the tracks of the Yamanote line. It's a cool little shopping street where beautiful handicrafts made from leather, wood, lacquer and ceramic are sold. However, these objects are not sedate and traditional – everything here has a modern touch! *Depending on the shop, usually Thur–Tue 11am–7pm | 5–9-23 Ueno | 5–9-23 上野 | Taitō-ku | 台東区 | www.jrtk.jp/2k540 | Subway G 14 Suehirocho | Suburban railway Okachimachi*

BENGARA (べんがら) (133 F2) (*S2*)

In this lovely shop within sight of the Sensoji temple, you can find many tradition-

Mitsukoshi: The venerable flagship among Tokyo's department stores

al accessories that decorate Japanese homes. *Open daily 10am–6pm | 1–35-6 Asakusa | 1–35-6 赤坂 | Taitō-ku | 台東区 | Subway G 19, A 18 Asakusa*

INSIDER TIP BINGOYA (備後屋) (131 D4) (*H4*)

The number one source for Japanese folk art, Bingoya presents five storeys full of useful and beautiful items made of ceramic, cloth or bamboo, as well as textiles, glassware and handmade paper. *Tue–Sun 10am–7pm; closed on the 3rd weekend of each month | 10–6 Wakamatsucho | 10–6 若松町 | Shinjuku-ku | 新宿区 | Subway E 03 Wakamatsu-Kawada*

HARA SHOBŌ (原書房) ★ (132 B4) (*N4*)

Large selection of coloured, Japanese

woodcuts from the 17th to the 20th centuries as well as modern prints. If you are looking for something specific, the staff speak English. *Tue–Sat 10am–6pm | 2–3 Kanda Jimbōchō | 2–3 神保町 | Chiyoda-ku | 千代田区 | www.harashobo.com/english | Subway Z 07, I 10, S 06 Jimbōchō*

ITŌYA (伊東屋) ★ (136 C2) (*⋒ O8*)

An institution since 1904: spread across three buildings on 18 floors, you can find a large selection of beautiful *washi* paper as well as calligraphy brushes, ink, small leather goods and unique pocket diaries. *Mon–Sat 10am–8pm, Sun 10am–7pm | 2–7-15 Ginza | 2–7-15 銀座 | Chūo-ku | 中央区 | Subway G 09, M 16 Ginza*

JAPAN SWORD (日本刀剣)

(136 A3) (*⋒ M9*)

Some of the old samurai swords here fetch upwards of £9,000/$12,000 – 40 times the price of a new one. Samurai helmets are also available. *Mon–Fri 9:30am–6pm, Sat 9:30am–5pm | 3–8-1 Toranomon | 3–8-1 虎ノ門 | Minato-ku | 港区 | www.japansword.co.jp | Subway G 07 Toranomon*

KYŪKYODŌ (鳩居堂)

(136 C2) (*⋒ O8*)

This shop offers embellished Japanese *washi* paper in the form of decorations, wrapping paper or greeting cards. Also available is the finest quality calligraphy paper, dusted with gold powder (approx. £130/$175 per sheet) as well as brushes and ink sticks. On the first floor you can find exquisite perfume oils, incense sticks and other items to delight your sense of smell. Founded in Kyoto in 1663 and relocated to Tokyo in 1880, Kyūkyodō is the former incense purveyor to the imperial household and is one of Ginza's tradition-bearers. *Mon–Sat 10am–7pm, Sun and holidays 11am–7pm | 5–7-4 Ginza | 5–7-4 銀座 | Chūo-ku | 中央区 | Subway G 09, M 16 Ginza*

INSIDER TIP ▶ TANAGOKORO (掌) Ⓥ

(136 C2) (*⋒ O8*)

Minimalist, organic and effective: the only product you can buy in this shop is white charcoal *(binchotan)*. Laboriously obtained from *ubame* oak wood, this charcoal takes the place of air fresheners or water filters. On the second floor, you can enjoy an exquisite tea and small snacks; fine whiskey is served in the cellar. *Mon–Fri 11am–8pm, Sat and Sun 11am–7pm | 1–8-15 Ginza | 1–8-15 銀座 | Chūo-ku | 中央区 | Subway Y 19 Ginza-Itchome*

FASHION

FROM 1ST (フロムファースト) ★

(134 C3) (*⋒ G10*)

A house with history: Japan's fashion gurus Issey Miyake, Rei Kawakubo and Yohji Yamamoto opened their first boutiques here. Today, up-and-coming designers set the tone. *Individual boutique hours vary | 5–3-10 Minami-Aoyama | 5–3-10 南青山 | Minato-ku | 港区 | Subway C 04, G 02, Z 02 Omotesandō*

INSIDER TIP ▶ JÜRGEN LEHL (ヨーガンレール) (136 B1) (*⋒ N8*)

The German fashion designer Jürgen Lehl has made a name for himself in Japan with his timeless and beautiful collections for men and women. *Open daily 11am–8pm | Shin Kokusai Bldg. 1F | 3–4-1 Marunouchi | 3–4-1 丸の内 | Chiyoda-ku | 千代田区 | Subway Y 18, H 07 Yūrakuchō*

LAFORET HARAJUKU (ラフォーレ原宿) (134 B2–3) (*⋒ F9*)

This fashion department store is popular among young, fashion-conscious Jap-

anese shoppers. Lots of cool shops from well-established as well as new fashion labels. *Open daily 11am–9pm | 1–11-6 Jingūmae | 1–11-6 神宮前 | Shibuya-ku | 渋谷区 | Subway C 03, F 15 Meiji-jingūmae*

INSIDER TIP **UNIQLO (**ユニクロ**)**
(136 C2) (*መ O8*)

Chic, inexpensive, but still excellent quality – Uniqlo has established itself as a fashion brand. The new, 12-storey flag-

Don't just walk past! Uniqlo has fashionable, wearable garments for everyone.

PARCO (パルコ)
(134 B3) (*መ E10*)

Young and innovative fashion. Parco 1 and 3 are also popular for their inexpensive lunch restaurant. Parco 1 offers free Wi-Fi. *Open daily 10am–9pm | 15–1 Udagawacho| 15–1 宇田川町 | Shibuya-ku | 渋谷区 | Subway G 01, Z 01, F 16 Shibuya | Yamanote loop line Shibuya*

SHIBUYA 109
(渋谷109)
(134 B4) (*መ E10*)

There are about 100 of these teenager-centric boutiques carrying the very latest trends. *Open daily 10am–9pm | 2–29-1 Dogenzaka | 2–29-1 道玄坂 | Shibuya-ku | 渋谷区 | Subway G 01, Z 01, F 16 Shibuya | Yamanote loop line Shibuya*

ship store in Ginza is a true shopping experience. There are several tax-free counters and some employees speak several languages. *Open daily 11am–9pm | 6–9-5 Ginza |6–9-5 銀座 | Chūō-ku | 中央区 | Subway G 09, M 16 Ginza*

PEARLS

MIKIMOTO (ミキモト) ★
(136 C2) (*መ O8*)

Mikimoto is by far the finest pearl dealership in the city. Its famous name guarantees first-class quality, and this comes at a price. In 1893, its founding father, Kōkichi Mikimoto, became the first person to successfully cultivate pearls. *Open daily 11am–7pm | 2–4-12 Ginza | 2–4-12 銀座 | Chūō-ku | 中央区 | www.mikimoto.com/en/index.html | Subway G 09, M 16 Ginza*

ENTERTAINMENT

Night-time Tokyo isn't just for business people: students and young office workers join in the mix.

Japan's capital is the perfect place to turn night into day. All of the uniformly dressed office workers who hurry, stoney-face to work in the mornings know how to party hard once the working day is done. Tokyo's large foreign community is also an integral part of its nightlife. Nevertheless, foreigners don't fit in everywhere. Occasionally, even rules apply: *Japanese only*. In that case, you should accept it. The range of entertainment is marked by internationality and local colour – from traditional Kabuki and Noh performances to pop concerts or classical music with world-class performers. Tokyo offers jazz cellars and clubs as well as countless venues for karaoke. Well-known British and American bands also perform in small concert halls

Sleepless in Tokyo: If you miss the last train, you can simply keep on partying. In Tokyo, there's always something going on.

(www.tokyogigguide.com). If you like things cosier, there are also plenty of pubs and bars.

BARS

BAR SIX (バーシス) ★ ⚓
(133 F2) (ᗰ S1)
This 6th-floor bar and terrace is a wonderful place to relax with a good wine and some snacks – plus a beautiful view of the Asakusa Kannon Temple (illuminated at night) and the Tokyo Skytree. *Tue–Sun 6pm–2am | 2–34-3 Asakusa | 2–34-3 浅 草 | Taito-ku | 台東区 | Subway G 19, A18 Asakusa*

HARD ROCK CAFE (ハードロックカフェ) (135 E3) (ᗰ K10)
For all those who still know who Jimi Hendrix is. In trendy Tokyo, the Hard Rock Cafe remains devoted to good old rock music. *Sun–Thur 11:30am–2am, Fri and Sat 11:30am–4am | 5–4-20 Roppongi | 5–4-20 六本木 | Minato-ku | 港区 | www.hardrock. com | Subway H 04, E 23 Roppongi*

Looking for a cool blonde?
You can find one in any bar!

INSIDER TIP PINK COW (ピンクカウ)

(135 E3) *(ⓜ K10)*

This bar's California-style concept is especially popular with Tokyo's large foreign community. Wi-Fi available. *Open daily 5pm–8am | 5–5-1 Roppongi | 5–5-1 六本木 | Minato-ku | 港区 | Subway H 04, E 23 Roppongi*

PROPAGANDA (プロパガンダ)

(135 E3) *(ⓜ K10)*

A popular Roppongi hangout for foreigners; usually it's already full by happy hour. Techno music and more; no cover charge. *Mon–Fri 6pm–5am Sat and Sun 7pm–5am | Yua Roppongi Building 2F | 3–14-9 Roppongi | 3–14-9 六本木 | Minato-ku | 港区 | www.propaganda-tokyo.com/english/index.html | Subway H 04, E 23 Roppongi*

SUPERDELUXE (スーパーデラックス)

★ (135 E4) *(ⓜ J10)*

More of an artists' salon than a bar. Its cult event, *Pecha Kucha*, takes place on the last Wednesday of each month: eight to 14 people present their architecture and design ideas using a maximum of 20 PowerPoint slides lasting 20 seconds each. It's best to check the website, since the bar is occasionally closed. *Usually open 6pm–1am | B1F | 3–1-25 Nishi-Azabu | 3–1-25 西麻布 | Minato-ku | 港区 | www.super-deluxe.com | Subway H 04, E 23 Roppongi*

THREE HUNDRED BAR 5 CHOME (300BAR スリーハンドレッドバー 銀座⑧丁目店) (136 C2) *(ⓜ O8)*

This small stand-up bar in the middle of Ginza is a place where secretaries and young office workers meet before going on to dinner. *Nomen est omen*: all drinks cost ¥300 plus VAT. A minimum purchase of two drink coupons is required; if you buy ten, you get one free. *Mon–Thur, Sun, holidays 5pm–2am, Fri, Sat and days before holidays 5pm–4am | 5–9-11 Ginza | 5–9-11 銀座 | Chūō-ku | 中央区 | www.300bar.com/english | Subway G 09, M 16, H 08 Ginza*

BEER HALLS

Conviviality in Japanese – beer consumption here is considerable, particularly in the summer, when even dignified department stores set up INSIDER TIP beer gardens on their rooftops and the atmosphere can become quite boisterous. One example is the Tokyu Honten in Shibuya. Absolutely worth a visit!

KIRIN CITY (キリンシティ)

(134 B4) *(ⓜ E10)*

Here you can drink a civilised beer in a relaxing atmosphere. There are about 25 of these pump rooms in Tokyo – for example, in Shibuya. *Mon–Sat noon–11:30pm, Sun 11:30am–11:30pm | Matsubara Bldg. 1F | 2–25-13 Dogenzaka*

*Shibuya | 2–25-13 道玄坂 | Shibuya-ku |
渋谷 | Subway G 01, M 16, F 16 Shibuya |
Yamanote loop line Shibuya*

LION (ビヤホールライオン 銀座七丁目店) (136 C2) (*Ø O8*)

One of Tokyo's oldest beer halls, this place has been serving drinks since 1934. Worth a visit more for the relaxed, informal atmosphere than for the food. *Open daily 11:30am–11pm | 7–9-20 Ginza | 7–9-20 銀座 | Chūō-ku | 中央区 | Subway G 09, M 16 Ginza*

DANCE CLUBS

AGEHA (アゲハ) ★ (139 E2) (*Ø e2*)

One of the largest clubs in Asia: the main dance floor accommodates over 2000 people, and the sound and lighting systems are excellent. The party mood extends to three additional dance floors, four bars, three VIP rooms and a pool. The only downside is that this gem of a club is located on the outskirts of Tokyo. Free shuttle buses leave from Shibuya

from 11pm. Tickets can be purchased on the bus; more information at *www.ageha. com* (links to schedules and accessibility!). *2–2-10 Shinkiba | 2–2-10 新木場 | Koto-ku | 江東区 | Subway Y 24 Shinkiba*

CONTACT (コンタクト) (134 A–B4) (*Ø E10*)

The managers of the now-defunct cult club *Air* – featured in the film *Lost in Translation* – have repeated their successful formula. Events with international DJs; minimum age 20 (IDs necessary!) *Opening times vary | Shin-Taiso Bldg. No. 4 B2 | 新大宗ビル4号館 B2F | 2–10-12 Dogenzaka | 2–10-12 道玄坂 | Shibuya-ku | 渋谷区 | www.contacttokyo.com | Subway G 01, Z 01, F 16 Shibuya | Yamanote loop line Shibuya*

DJ BAR BRIDGE (ディジェイ バー ブリジ) (134 B4) (*Ø F10*)

A mixture of bar and club for fans of cocktails and danceable music. There's also a fantastic view of the famous Shibuya Crossing! *Sat, Mon–Fri 8pm–5am, Sun 6pm–*

★ **Bar Six**
Relaxation Tokyo style: fine wines and a superb view of the Asakusa Kannon Temple → p. 85

★ **SuperDeluxe**
A very hip mixture of bar and salon for artists and other creative types → p. 86

★ **Ageha**
Gigantic dance floors, multiple bars, excellent sound and even a pool: this mega-club is simply mega-good. → p. 87

★ **Abbey Road**
For fans of the legendary Fab Four. Some of the Beatles impersonators are even better than the originals. → p. 89

★ **Blue Note Tokyo**
Another very good imitation – this time, of New York's Blue Note jazz club: the finest in jazz → p. 89

★ **National Theatre**
For lovers of the Japanese classical arts: from traditional music and dance to kabuki theatre → p. 91

MARCO POLO HIGHLIGHTS

midnight | Admission ¥1000 | Park Side Kyoudou Bldg. 1OF | 渋谷パークサイド共同ビル10F | 1–25-6 Shibuya | 1–25-6 渋谷 | Shibuyaku | 渋谷区 | www.bridge-shibuya.com | Subway G 01, Z 01, F 16 Shibuya | Yamanote loop line Shibuya

SOUND MUSEUM VISION
(サウンド　ミュージアム　ビジョン) (134 A4) (🏛 E10)

The mostly young clientele fills four rooms, dancing to music ranging from rock to techno; excellent sound system.

LOW BUDGET

Via *meetup.com*, you can quickly find like-minded people for evening activities – for example, for a communal cooking evening, lectures or wine-tasting.

For an evening at the cinema, *Ladies Day* – usually Wednesdays – is a good option. Then tickets for women usually cost around £6/$9 and on the first day of each month, this price applies to everyone.

Hang out on the artificial beach in Odaiba (139 E3) (🏛 e3): there's low-priced evening entertainment from May to October. Buy your food and drink at the *Maruetsu* supermarket (directly in front of the Yurikamome Station Odaiba-kaihinkōen).

Take advantage of Happy Hour at some top hotels – for example, *Mon–Sat 5pm–8pm* at the *Champagne Bar* of the *Ana Intercontinental Tokyo* (135 F3) (🏛 L9) (1–12-33 Akasaka | Minato-ku |Subway N 06, G 06 Tameike-Sannō).

Women have free admission on "Girls Festival" days. IDs checked for some events. *Open daily 8pm–late | Price of admission varies | 2–10-7 Dogenzaka | 2–10-7 道玄坂 | Shibuya-ku | 渋谷区 | www.vision-tokyo.com | Subway G 01, Z 01, F 16 Shibuya | Yamanote loop line Shibuya*

INSIDER TIP ▶ WOMB (ウーム)
(134 A4) (🏛 E10)

A super club for weekends with great DJs on several dance floors and fabulous light and laser shows. Usually only one dance floor is open on weekdays. Admission prices and programmes vary! *2–16 Maruyama-cho | 2–16 円山町 | Shibuya-ku | 渋谷区 | www.womb.co.jp | Subway G 01, Z 01, F 16 Shibuya | Yamanote loop line Shibuya*

KARAOKE

The chain venues *Big Echo*, *Karaokekan* and *Shidax* have numerous locations and offer a good selection of English-language songs.

SHIDAX ROPPONGI CLUB
(シダックス六本木クラブ) ●
(135 E3) (🏛 K10)

Here you can sing in karaoke suites with designer décor. Songs – in English and other European languages – can be selected by remote control. *Mon–Fri 5pm–5am, Sat and Sun 2pm–5am | Rates vary according to room size and time of day | 5-2-4 Roppongi | 5–2-4 六本木 | Minato-ku | 港区 | Tel. 03 54 74 11 22 | Subway H 04, E 23 Roppongi*

TEMPLE OF CULTURE

BUNKAMURA (文化村ら) ●
(134 A4) (🏛 E10)

In this massive cultural complex containing a museum, gallery and arthouse cinema, the Cocoon theatre pre-

Unobtrusive on the outside, rocking on the inside: A karaoke bar in Shibuya

sents first-class concerts, musicals and ballet performances. The gallery holds changing exhibitions, from Flemish masters to contemporary Japanese art. A French café is located in the atrium. The INSIDER TIP *art house cinema* on the 6th floor primarily shows European films, often in their original languages with subtitles or in English. On Tuesdays and on Sunday evenings, tickets cost only ¥1000. *2–24-1 Dogenzaka | 2–24-1 道玄坂 | Shibuya-ku | 渋谷区 | Tel. 03 34 77 91 11 | www.bunkamura.co.jp/english/index.html | Subway G 01, Z 01, F 16 Shibuya | Yamanote loop line Shibuya*

LIVEMUSIK

ABBEY ROAD (アビーロード) ★
(135 E3) (𝄞 K9)

The best Fab Four impersonators in Tokyo are probably the Parrots. At Abbey Road, they and other bands also play numbers that were never in the Beatles' Liverpool repertoire. Unfortunately there is no dance floor. Minimum purchase of two drinks or one drink plus a meal. *Mon–Thur 6pm–11:30pm, Fri, Sat and before public holidays 6pm–midnight | Admission starting at ¥2000 | Roppongi Bldg. Annex B1 | 4–11-5 Roppongi | 4–11-5 六本木 | Minato-ku | 港区 | Tel. 03 34 02 00 17 | www.abbeyroad.ne.jp | Subway H 04, E 23 Roppongi*

INSIDER TIP BAUHAUS (バウハウス)
(134 E3) (𝄞 J9–10)

An outstanding cover band plays stadium rock with humour and gusto – from Deep Purple to Queen through to Bon Jovi and Guns N' Roses – in a jazz bar atmosphere. Anyone who wants to can rock along on-stage! A hefty price (¥3000), but the band plays several sets, and you will leave in a great mood. *Mon–Sat 7pm–1am | 5–3-4 Roppongi | 5–3-4 六本木 | Minato-ku | 港区 | www.ebauhaus.jp | Subway H 04, E 23 Roppongi*

BLUE NOTE TOKYO (ブルーノート東京) ★ (134 C3) (𝄞 H10)

Experience Dizzy Gillespie, Sarah Vaughan or Sergio Mendez up close and personal in this faithful copy of the famous New York jazz club. Capacity limited to 200 guests. Good but expensive. *Closed sporadically, otherwise Mon–Fri 5:30pm–midnight, live music starting at 7pm; Sat and Sun 3:30pm–11pm | Admission from ¥7000 | Leica Bldg. | 6–3-16 Minami-Aoyama | 6–3-16 南青山 | Minato-ku | 港区 | Tel. 03 54 85 00 88 | www.bluenote.co.jp | Subway G 02, C 04, Z 02 Omotesandō*

LIQUID ROOM (リキッドルーム)
(134 C5) (*ϺϽ G12*)

Live performances by international and local bands and DJs. Performances end before midnight! Admission can be expensive, but the popular café bar is free. *3–16-6 Higashi |3–16-6 東 | Shibuya-ku | 渋谷区 | Tel. 03 54 64 08 00 | www. liquidroom.net | Subway H 02 Ebisu | Yamanote loop line Ebisu*

PIT-INN (ピットイン)
(130 B5) (*ϺϽ F5*)

Jazz club with good music and realistic prices. Newcomers play in the afternoons. *Open daily 2pm–5pm and 7:30pm–10:30pm | Admission: afternoons from ¥1200 (incl. 1 drink), eve-*

nings from ¥3000 | Akōdo Shinjuku Bldg. B1 | 2–12-4 Shinjuku | 2–12-4 新宿 | Shinjukuku | 新宿区 | Tel. 03 33 54 20 24 | www.pit-inn.com | Subway M 09, S 02 Shinjukusanchōme

LOVE HOTELS

If you travel to Tokyo with a partner, you shouldn't miss the chance to experience the **INSIDER TIP** wonderfully kitschy love

TIME TO CHILL

After a long day of walking, a bath at a sentō, a neighbourhood bath house, feels especially good. In these tradition-steeped locations, men and women always bathe separately – and nude. Sentōs are intended for personal hygiene and relaxation, but they also have a social and spiritual function. A daily bath is part of Japan's culture of cleanliness. You can only go into the water after a thorough scrubbing out-side the pool. Soap and towels are usually available for a fee. Caution: the water temperature of about 42 °C/108 °F requires that you enter slowly. Try ● *Take-no-yu Onsen* (135 E5) (*ϺϽ K11*) *(Tue–Sun 3:30pm–11:30pm | Admission approx. £3.50/$5 | 1–15-12 Minami-Azabu | Minato-ku | Subway N 04, O 22 Azabujuban)*. This bath is known for the high mineral content of its water, which is considered particularly relaxing.

Inspired by the famous New York club: Listen to the finest jazz music at the Blue Note Tokyo.

hotels. These are nothing like bordellos – a kyūkei (a rest) starts at £40/$50 for two hours and a tomari (overnight stay) starts at £95/$130. The hotels offer nearly every type of ambience – from a love nest with a waterbed to jungle-themed room. *Shibuya (130 A–B4) (ɯ E10)* is a good address to start with. From the *109 department store*, walk downhill on the Dogenzaka and turn right after approx. 200 m/220 yd. The hotels display signs reading "rest" and "stay".

DANCE & THEATRE

KABUKI-ZA (歌舞伎座) ●
(136 C2) *(ɯ O8–9)*

For several years now, the ancient art of Kabuki theatre has been revived here. The multi-act performances combining song, pantomime and dance last for several hours. If you want to simply get a taste, it's best to inquire at the box office about a INSIDER TIP *Hitomaku-mi* – a ticket for just one act. *4–12-15 Ginza | 4–12-15 銀座 | Chūo-ku | 中央区 | www.kabuki-bito.jp/eng/top.html | Subway HO9, A 11 Higashi-Ginza*

NATIONAL NOH THEATRE (国立能劇場)
(134 C1) *(ɯ F–G7)*

It is only very recently that women have also been allowed to participate in this theatre form, which dates back to the 14th century. The dramas often draw on mythological sources and the performances are very formal. You can experience a piece of Japanese cultural history here. *Performance times vary | Admission from £20/$25 | 4–18-1 Sendagaya | 4–18-1 千駄ヶ谷 | Shibuya-ku | 渋谷区 | Ticket sales tel. (English) 03 34 23 13 31 | www.ntj.jac.go.jp/english | Subway E 25 Kokuritsukyōgijō | Suburban railway Sobu Sendagaya*

NATIONAL THEATRE (国立劇場) ★
(135 F1) *(ɯ L7)*

Performances of Kabuki, Bunraku, classical Japanese music, classical courtly dance and religious singing. *Performance times vary | Admission from £11/$15 | 4–1 Hayabusa-cho | 4–1 隼町 | Chiyoda-ku | 千代田区 | Ticket sales tel. 03 32 65 74 11 | www.ntj.jac.go.jp/english | Subway Z 05 Hanzōmon*

WHERE TO STAY

In Tokyo, you have the choice between a hotel room equipped with beds in the familiar Western style or sleeping the traditional Japanese way at an inn known as a ryokan. Here, you sleep on rice-straw tatami mats, where thin futon mattresses are laid out in the evenings. It's important to know that at lower price categories in Japanese lodgings, toilets and baths are shared between several rooms. *Business hotels* also offer inexpensive lodging in rooms that are frequently very small but clean. Prices at top hotels are comparable to those in other major cities. In general, the tourism boom in Tokyo has pushed prices upward, and available rooms are scarce, so it's best to book well in advance.

Some online booking platforms allow you to cancel free of charge at short notice. Be sure to double-check whether the price is applied per room or per person.

HOTELS: EXPENSIVE

IMPERIAL HOTEL (帝国ホテル東京)
(136 B2) (*∅ N8*)

The Imperial Hotel, located near the Imperial Palace, has been welcoming guests from all over the world since 1890. While the exterior of the present building – the third in the hotel's history – does not have the same grandeur as its predecessors, its service, comfort and flair are still fit for an emperor. A very special attraction, that is also available to non-guests, is the private ● **INSIDER TIP** *tea ceremony (Reserve by phone: 03 35 04*

A familiar bed or a typical futon?
Sleeping in traditional Japanese style
at a ryokan is always worth a try.

11 11 | approx. £15/$20). It's performed by masters of this traditional art and takes place in the hotel's tea ceremony rooms on the 4th floor. *931 rooms | 1–1-1 Uchi-saiwai-cho | 1-1-1 内幸町 | Chiyoda-ku | 千代田区 |*
Tel. 03 35 04 11 11 | www.imperialhotel. co.jp/e | Subway I 08, C 09, H 07 Hibiya

NEW ŌTANI (ホテルニューオータニ)
🌐 **(135 E1)** (*∅ K7*)

This gigantic, three-building hotel complex is a sort of city within the city. It in-
cludes a beautiful Japanese garden built in the 16th century. In the summer you can dive into the outdoor swimming pool and its restaurants and shopping arcades are full of lively comings and goings. The hotel is operated sustainably, with its own well and water treatment plant, a landscaped roof and biotopes in the garden. *1479 rooms | 4–1 Kioi-cho | 4–1 紀尾井町 | Chiyodaku | 千代田区 | Tel. 03 32 65 11 11 | www.newotanihotels.com | Subway G 05, M 13 Akasaka-mitsuke*

Elegant and classically Japanese:
The interior does not disappoint

fia Coppola's film *Lost in Translation*. *177 rooms and suites | 3–7–1–2 Nishi-Shinjuku | 3–7–1–2 西新宿 | Shinjuku-ku | 新宿区 | Tel. 03 53 22 12 34 | www.tokyo.park. hyatt.com | Yamanote loop line Shinjuku | Subway M 08 Shinjuku*

THE TOKYO STATION HOTEL (東京ス テーションホテル) (136 C1) *(Ⅲ O7)*
A history-steeped hotel with a classical European ambiance and first-class Japanese service. Located directly adjacent to the central railway station, it makes the perfect base for exploring the city. *150 rooms | 1–9–1 Marunouchi | 1–9–1 丸の内 | Chiyoda-ku | 千代田区 | Tel. 03 52 20 11 11 | www. thetokyostationhotel.jp | Subway M 17 Tokyo | Yamanote loop line Tokyo*

HOTELS: MODERATE

ANA INTERCONTINENTAL TOKYO (インターコンチネンタル東京) ★ ❧ (135 F3) *(Ⅲ L9)*
This hotel is part of a building complex that includes the Suntory Hall, one of Tokyo's most beautiful concert halls. The nightclub districts of Roppongi and Akasaka are within walking distance. *844 rooms | 1–12–33 Akasaka | 1–12–33 赤坂 | Minato-ku | 港区 | Tel. 03 35 05 11 11 | www.anaintercontinental-tokyo.jp/e | Subway N 06, G 06 Tameike-Sannō*

HOTEL OKURA TOKYO (ホテルオーク ラ東京) ★ (135 F3) *(Ⅲ L9)*
This luxury hotel has enjoyed an excellent reputation among foreigners for 50 years. It is characterised by its dignified elegance and impeccable service; almost a bargain in this category. *796 rooms | 2–10–4 Toranomon | 2–10–4 虎ノ門 | Minato-ku | 港区 | Tel. 03 35 82 01 11 | www. hotelokura.co.jp/tokyo/en | Subway H 05 Kamiyachō*

PARK HYATT TOKYO (パークハイア ット東京) ❧ (130 A6) *(Ⅲ D6)*
A popular top-class hotel housed in a skyscraper designed by Kenzō Tange. It was made famous as the location for So-

ASAKUSA VIEW HOTEL (浅草ビュー ホテル) (133 E2) *(Ⅲ R2)*
If you're looking for a comfortable stay in the old part of Tokyo, you've come to the right place. ❧ 20 m/65 ft pool on the 5th floor with a view of the traditional neighbourhood. *337 rooms | 3–17–1 Nishi-Asakusa | 3–17–1 西浅草 | Taitō-ku | 台 東区 | Tel. 03 38 47 11 11 | www.viewhotels. co.jp/asakusa | Subway G 18 Tawaramachi | Suburban railway Tsukuba Express Asakusa*

10

CRESTON HOTEL (クレストンホテル)
★ (134 A3) (*E10*)

An unobtrusive-looking hotel on a quiet side street just a few minutes from the bustle of Shibuya, Yoyogi Park and the Meiji Shrine. Free Wi-Fi, helpful personnel and a fair price, with an excellent *shabu-shabu* restaurant on the ground floor. *53 rooms | 10–8 Kamiyama-cho | 10–8 神山町 | Shibuya-ku | 渋谷区 | Tel. 03 34 81 58 00 | www.crestonhotel.jp/shibuya | Yamanote loop line Shibuya | Subway Z 01, G 01 Shibuya*

KEIO PLAZA HOTEL (京王プラザホテル) ⚓ (130 A5) (*E5*)

A reliable hotel with comparatively large rooms, fantastic views (Mt. Fuji!) and a rooftop pool. There's a **INSIDER TIP** free shuttle bus to Tokyo Disneyland, which makes it a good choice for families. *1435 rooms | 2–2-1 Nishi-Shinjuku | 2–2-1 西新宿 | Shinjukuku | 新宿区 | Tel. 03 33 44 01 11 |www.keioplaza.com/index.html | Subway M 08 Shinjuku | Yamanote loop line Shinjuku*

MERCURE GINZA (メルキュールホテル銀座東京) ★ (136 C2) (*O8*)

Located on quiet side street in the Ginza shopping district, this hotel is an ideal starting point for exploring the city. The Fish Market, Kabuki Theatre and Imperial Palace are all easily reachable on foot, as are countless restaurants. The hotel personnel speak good English. *208 rooms | 2–9-4 Ginza | 2–9-4 銀座 | Chuo-ku | 中央区 |Tel. 03 43 35 11 11 | www.mercure.com/gb/hotel-5701-mercure-tokyo-ginza/index.shtml | Subway Y 19 Ginza-itchōme*

RICHMOND HOTEL PREMIER ASAKUSA INTERNATIONAL (リッチモンドホテルプレミア浅草インターナショナル) (133 F2) (*R2*)

Newly opened in 2015, this branch of a nationwide hotel chain is geared towards international guests with the staff speaking multiple languages. Good location: the Asakusa Kannon Temple is right around the corner. The non-smoking rooms are fairly large by Japanese standards. *270 rooms | 2–6-7 Asakusa | 2–6-7 浅草 |*

MARCO POLO HIGHLIGHTS

Taito-ku | 台東区 | Tel. 03 58 06 31 55 | asakusa-international.richmondhotel.jp | Subway A 18, G 19 Asakusa

HOTEL SUNROUTE PLAZA SHINJUKU (ホテル　サンルートプラザ　新宿) (130 B6) (*∭ E6*)

This classic upper-class *business hotel* is just a few minutes away from Shinjuku Station. Another plus point: the personnel are experienced in dealing with foreigners. *624 rooms | 2–3-1 Yoyogi | 2–3-1 代々木 | Shibuya-ku | 渋谷区 | Tel. 03 33 75 32 11 |*

LUXURY HOTELS

Conrad Tokyo ☙ **(136 B3)** (*∭ N9–10*)
Lxury hotel on the 28th–37th floors of the Tokyo Shiodome Tower skyscraper. Here, classical elegance harmonises with Japanese design elements. 290 rooms and suites, starting at approx. £300/$400. *1–9-1 Higashi-Shimbashi | Minato-ku | Tel. 03 63 88 80 00 | www.conradtokyo.co.jp | Subway E 19 Shiodome*

Four Seasons Hotel Tokyo at Marunouchi ☙ **(136 C1)** (*∭ O7*)
Exclusive ambience, very large rooms and excellent service make this hotel stand out. Located directly adjacent to Tokyo's central railway station. 57 rooms and suites, starting at approx. £450/$615. *Pacific Century Place | 1–11-1 Marunouchi | Chiyoda-ku | Tel. 03 52 22 72 22 | www.fourseasons.com/tokyo | Subway M 17 Tōkyō | Suburban railway lines Tōkyō*

Grand Hyatt Tokyo ☙ **(135 E4)** (*∭ J10*)
Ideal location in the Roppongi Hills complex. The liveliest of Tokyo's luxury hotels has 387 rooms and suites, starting at approx. £325/$430. *6–10-3 Roppongi | Minato-ku | Tel. 03 43 33 12 34 | www.tokyo.grand.hyatt.com | Subway H 04, E 23 Roppongi*

Mandarin Oriental Tokyo ☙ **(132 D6)** (*∭ P6*)
A direct neighbour of the venerable Mitsukoshi department store and close to the business and finance districts. Elegant interior and excellent service. 157 rooms and 21 suites, starting at approx. £410/$550. *2–1-1 Nihonbashi-Muromachi | Chūo-ku | Tel. 03 32 70 88 00 | www.mandarinoriental.com/tokyo | Subway Z 09 Mitsukoshimae*

The Peninsula Tokyo ☙ **(136 B2)** (*∭ N8*)
A worthy representative of this luxury chain near the Imperial Palace. The hotel even has a heliport and its automobile fleet includes a 1934 Rolls Royce Phantom II. 267 rooms and 47 suites, starting at approx. £410/$550. *1–8-1 Yūraku-cho | Chiyoda-ku | Tel. 03 62 70 28 88 | tokyo.peninsula.com | Subway I 08, C 09, H 07 Hibiya*

The Ritz-Carlton ☙ **(135 E3)** (*∭ J9*)
Super luxurious! 248 rooms and suites occupy the 45th to 53rd floors of the Midtown complex in Roppongi; prices start at approx. £350/$470. *Tokyo Midtown | 9–7-1 Akasaka | Minato-ku | Tel. 03 34 23 80 00 | www.ritzcarlton.com | Subway H 04, E 23 Roppongi*

In the Roppongi Hills skyscraper complex: The Sky Lounge of the luxurious Grand Hyatt Tokyo

www.hotelsunrouteplazashinjuku.jp/ en | Subway M 08 Shinjuku | Yamanote loop line Shinjuku

THE B ROPPONGI (ザ・ビー六本木) (135 E3) (⑳ K9)

This middle-class hotel is popular among foreign visitors and Japanese businesspeople alike. The breakfast buffet offers something for every taste and internet is available free of charge. The best part is its central location in Roppongi allowing you to get to Roppongi Hills and Midtown in no time. *65 rooms | 3–9-8 Roppongi | 3–9-8 六本木 | Minato-ku | 港区 | Tel. 03 54 12 04 51 | www.thebhotels.com | Subway H 04, E 23 Roppongi*

HOTEL VILLA FONTAINE (ホテルビラ ホンテーヌ) (135 F3) (⑳ L9)

This elegant hotel in Roppongi is not just for night owls. It belongs to a Tokyo-wide chain that offers good value for money. *189 rooms | 1–6-2 Roppongi | 1–6-2 六本木 | Minato-ku | 港区 | Tel. 03 35 60 11 10 | www.hvf.jp/eng/ roppongi.php | Subway N 05 Roppongi-itchōme*

YAMANOUE (HILLTOP) HOTEL (山の上ホテル) ★ (132 B4) (⑳ N4)

A hotel with unconventional charm. The rooms are furnished in a manner that is are reminiscent of 1950s Japan. Good restaurant and outstanding service. *74 rooms | 1–1 Kanda Surugadai | 1–1 神田 駿河台 | Chiyoda-ku | 千代田区 | Tel. 03 32 93 23 11 | www.yamanoue-hotel. co jp | Subway S 06, I 10, Z 07 Jimbōchō*

HOTELS: BUDGET

AJIA KAIKAN (WI) (ホテル　アジア 会館) ★ (135 E2) (⑳ J8)

This hotel, in a central yet quiet location, has recently been renovated. The rooms are small, but some have private bathrooms. The late check-out time of 12 noon is another plus point. Very good value for money. *172 rooms | 8–10-32 Akasaka | 8–10-32 赤坂 | Minato-ku | 港区 | Tel. 03 34 02 61 11 | www.asiacenter.or.jp | Subway Z 03, G 04 Aoyama-Itchōme*

INSIDER TIP ANDON RYOKAN (WI) (行燈旅館) (139 E2) (⑳ e2)

The modern and the traditional are optimally combined in a very small space.

This ryokan has 24 small rooms with laptop connections, TV and DVD players, showers and toilets on every floor. Smokers must step out onto the miniature terrace. While the location is somewhat impractical, the rooms are unrivalled value for the money. *2–34-10 Nihon-zutsumi | 2–34-10* 日本堤 *| Taito-ku |* 台東区 *| Tel. 03 38 73 86 11 | www.andon.co.jp | Subway H 19 Minowa*

ANNEX KATSUTARO RYOKAN (WI) (アネックス勝太郎旅館) ★
(139 E2) (ψ e2)

A ryokan in the Yanaka district offering spacious tatami-mat rooms with bathrooms, cotton kimonos, in-room internet connection and Wi-Fi in the lobby – all very inexpensively. This gem is also suitable for families as the largest room accommodates six people. Non-smoking rooms only. *17 rooms | 3–8-4 Yanaka | 3–8-4* 谷中 *| Taito-ku |* 台東区 *| Tel. 03 38 28 25 00 | www.katsutaro.com | Subway C 15 Sendagi*

FIRST CABIN TSUKIJI (ファーストキャビン築地) ★ (137 D3) (ψ P9)

This new version of a capsule hotel is compact yet stylish. The first-class cabins (4.4 m²/47 sq ft, bed 120 cm/47 in wide) for approx. £50/$70 also contain a small table. The business-class cabins (2.5 m²/27 sq ft, bed 100 cm/39 in wide) for £45/$60 have a shelf. In addition, there is a towel hire fee of approx. £0.60/$0.85. Short stays are also possible: one hour costs about £6/$8.50. *160 rooms | 2–11-10 Tsukiji | 2–11-10* 築地 *| Chūō-ku |* 中央区 *| Tel. 03 51 48 11 30 | www.firstcabin.jp.e.jr.hp.transer.com/locationlist/tsukiji.html | Subway H 10 Tsukiji*

KIMI RYOKAN (WI) (貴美旅館)
(139 E2) (ψ e2)

The 38 tatami rooms separated by thin partition walls are tiny but very clean. The atmosphere is more like a backpacker hostel than a ryokan. The roof terrace is a nice place to relax. *2–36-8 Ikebukuro | 2–36-8* 池袋 *| Toshima-ku |* 豊島区 *| Tel. 03 39 71 37 66 | www.kimiryokan.jp | Subway Y 09, M 25 Ikebukuro (west exit) | Yamanote loop line Ikebukuro (West exit)*

SAWANOYA RYOKAN (WI) (澤の屋旅館) ★ (132 C1) (ψ O1)

The Sawa family offers 12 tatami rooms in this very popular ryokan. Tea, instant coffee and information are free; breakfast is extra. Two of

LOW BUDGET

The pioneer among backpacker hotels (including rental bicycles) is the recommendable *Hotel New Koyo* (139 E2) (ψ e2) *(76 rooms | starting at £22/$30 | 2–26-3 Nihon-zutsumi | Taitō-ku | Tel. 03 38 73 03 43 | www.newkoyo.com | Subway H 19 Minowa).*

Welcome Inns (WI) are very tourist-friendly: these are smaller ryokan, guest houses and inexpensively-priced hotels *(www.japaneseinngroup.com).*

On Internet platforms such as *www.agoda.com* or *www.booking.com* you can sometimes find better prices than those offered directly by the hotel. If it seems to be sold out, or if you have special requests, it's best to phone.

the rooms have private baths while the others have sinks. There's also a shared bathroom. *2–3-11 Yanaka | 2–3-11 谷中 | Taitō-ku | 台東区 | Tel. 03 38 22 22 51 | www.sawanoya.com | Subway C 14 Nezu*

Subway G 19, A 18 Asakusa; Khaosan Tokyo Origami 3–4-12 Asakusa | 3–4-12 浅草 (133 F2) *(ᗰ S1) Taito-ku | 台東区 | Tel. 03 38 71 66 78 | Subway G 19, A 18 Asakusa; Khaosan Tokyo Laboratory 2–1-4 Nishiasakusa | 2–1-4 西浅草*

Not for the claustrophobic: Stylish cabins in the luxury capsule hotel First Cabin

BACKPACKER HOTELS

KHAOSAN TOKYO (カオサン東京) ⚉

The original branch of this successful chain of hostels is located directly on the Sumida River, with a lovely view of the Tokyo Skytree. There are a total of 35 beds and you can book one in a four-bed room for about £18/$25. The six new branches, such as the Origami, near the Asakusa Kannon Temple, are more colourful and modern, but also somewhat more expensive. *Khaosan Tokyo Original 2–1-5 Kaminarimon | 2–1-5 雷門* (133 F3) *(ᗰ S2) Taitō-ku | 台東区 | Tel. 03 38 42 82 86 |*

(133 E2) *(ᗰ R2) Taito-ku | 台東区 | Tel. 03 64 79 10 41 | Subway G 18 Tawaramachi | www.khaosan-tokyo.com*

WISE OWL HOSTEL
(ワイズ アウル ホステル) ★
(137 D2) *(ᗰ P8)*

A lot of class for little money: Taking up four storeys, this new hostel offers space in stylishly designed group, double and "family rooms" with high-quality memory foam mattresses that conform to the sleeper's anatomy. *118 rooms | 3–22-9 Hatchōbori | 3–22-9 八丁堀 | Chuo-ku | 中央区 | Tel. 03 55 41 29 60 | www.wiseowlhostels.com | Subway H 11 Hatchōbori*

DISCOVERY TOURS

① TOKYO AT A GLANCE

START: ① Fish Market
END: ⑭ Shibuya

1 day
Walking/driving time
(without stops)
4 hours

Distance:
➡ 40 km/25 miles

COSTS: Approx. ¥11,500 per person for day pass on subway, admission tickets, meals and taxi

WHAT TO PACK: Umbrella/sun hat, snacks and water

IMPORTANT TIPS: This tour is very quickly paced, so keep an eye on the time!

Even if you love to sleep late, make an effort to get up early today – it'll be worth it! From the world's largest fish market, idyllic parks and traditional

Would you like to explore the places that are unique to this city? Then the Discovery Tours are just the thing for you – they include terrific tips for stops worth making, breathtaking places to visit, selected restaurants and fun activities. It's even easier with the Touring App: download the tour with map and route to your smartphone using the QR Code on pages 2/3 or from the website address in the footer below – and you'll never get lost again even when you're offline.

TOURING APP

→ p. 2/3

shrines to breath-taking views across Tokyo's sea of houses and the nightlife of Shibuya, Japan's capital has it all.

07:00am Start with a visit to the bustling ❶ **Fish Mar-ket** → p. 49. Why not have some fish for breakfast? At the **Outer Market**, you can get the freshest sushi in the world – from scallops and eel to tuna. The selection is especially large at **Sushizanmai** *(open daily | 4–11-9 Tsukiji | Chuoku)*; the staff is accustomed to foreign guests.

❶ Fish Market

Photo: View from the Mori Tower

08:00am Take the subway to Meijijingumae. After a 15-minute walk through an old, tree-lined street, you will reach the tranquil **②** Meiji Shrine → p. 37. Do you want to try your luck with the Shinto gods? Then write your prayers or wishes on votive tablets or purchase a good luck charm.

② Meiji Shrine

10:00am After this contemplative stop, **walk on to Harajuku Station** and immerse yourself in the world of shopping. A stroll along Tokyo's luxurious boulevard of **③** Omotesandō → p. 37 takes you past the flagship stores of world-renowned designers. **At Omotesandō, you will cross the wide Aoyama-dori**. After taking in all of these impressions, it's the perfect time for a break. **Across from subway exit A4**, the scent of flowers and tea beckons from the **④** Aoyama Flower Market Tea House → p. 63. The rose parfait, made with real flower petals, is delicious.

③ Omotesandō

④ Aoyama Flower Market Tea House

11:30am From the teahouse, it's a seven-minute walk to the **⑤** Nezu-Museum → p. 39. This is worth a stop for three reasons: the ultra-modern museum building is a sight to behold; inside, you can immerse yourself in exotic East Asia

⑤ Nezu Museum

DISCOVERY TOURS

art; and the surrounding Japanese garden is an absolutely beautiful place.

12:30pm **Leave the museum on the left and turn into the first street on the right** to the unique ⑥ **INSIDER TIP** **Taro Okamoto Memorial Museum** *(Wed–Mon 10am–9pm | 6–1-19 Minamiaoyama | Minato-ku)*. This former studio belonging to the Japanese artist is hung with his gigantic paintings and in the garden you can marvel at his surrealistic sculptures. The scale is somewhat smaller **in the next side street on the left**, at ⑦ **Sou Sou Kyoto** *(Open daily 11am–8pm | 5–4-24 Aoyama| Minato-ku)*. Stock up on traditional printed items, such as a cloth bag or other beautiful gifts!

01:30pm Is your stomach rumbling? Satisfy it with a light organic lunch or snack and a soft-serve, vegan ice cream at ⑧ **Pure Deli & Store → p. 64. Afterwards, take a right turn back to Omotesandō Station. Take the subway to Shinjuku-Sanchōme, and leave the station through exit C5. To your right, follow the Shinjuku-dori to the next set of traffic lights.** Here, on your left, is the entrance to the expansive ⑨ **Shinjuku Imperial Gardens → p. 46**. Savour a walk through the beautiful park with its cherry trees and rose garden.

04:00pm Time to get back on the subway: from Shinjukugyoenmae Station, it's a 20-minute ride to Roppongi. Here, two gigantic buildings are the perfect shopping destinations. In the ⑩ **Tokyo Midtown → p. 43, The Cover Nippon** on the third floor offers beautiful handicrafts. The stylish **Idée Café Parc**, on the same level, is an ideal place for a break from shopping. Then, in **Roppongi Hills → p. 42**, you can soar to great heights: admission is not cheap, but from the observation deck of the 54-storey ⑪ **Mori Tower → p. 43**, you have the most beautiful view of Tokyo. When the weather is fine, you can take photographs from the open Sky Deck, unimpeded by glass. One floor below, at the **Mori Art Museum → p. 41**, you can experience how exciting modern art can be. You can buy curious and creative items in the museum shop.

07:00pm Time for dinner: ⑫ **Gonpachi → p. 69** is known for its lively atmosphere and grilled skewered meats. Do you love jazz? Then grab a taxi to the legendary club ⑬ **Blue Note Tokyo → p. 89**.

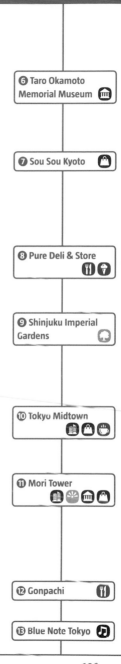

⑥ Taro Okamoto Memorial Museum

⑦ Sou Sou Kyoto

⑧ Pure Deli & Store

⑨ Shinjuku Imperial Gardens

⑩ Tokyo Midtown

⑪ Mori Tower

⑫ Gonpachi

⑬ Blue Note Tokyo

11:00pm The nightlife district of ⑭ **Shibuya** → p. 37 is buzzing with life until very late. Quickly navigate the world-famous **Shibuya Crossing** → p. 37 and then catch the last subways, which run until midnight. If you don't feel like sleeping, head for **Womb** → p. 88, one of the best techno clubs in the city, and dance the night away. Tired but happy, you can catch the first subway train at 5am.

⑭ Shibuya 🏢🍸🎵

2 SEE, SAIL AND SHOP

START: ① Tokyo Skytree END: ⑩ Ginza	1 day Walking time (without stops) 3 hours
Distance: ⊖ 18 km/11 miles	

🏢 🚇 🎏

🎎 🚲 🌳   **COSTS:** Approx. ¥8800 per person for rickshaw ride, ferry, admission tickets, meals and drinks

☕ 🛍 🚃   **WHAT TO PACK:** Umbrella/sun hat, water and snacks

🏛 🍴

On this tour, you can walk from the small streets of the old Asakusa district to the ultra-trendy designer district Ginza. You will never forget the view of this Japanese megacity from the highest platform of the Tokyo Skytree!

① Tokyo Skytree
🏢🎎☕

08:00am ① **Tokyo Skytree** → p. 53. From the second-highest building in the world, you can even see the elegant volcanic cone of Fuji-san, if the weather is clear → p. 57. Not afraid of heights? Then head for the lower **observation deck**! Through its glass floor, you have a sensational view 350 m/1150 feet downward. If you prefer secure seating, there are coffee and snacks at Japan's highest café, the **Skytree Café** *(Open daily 8am–9:45pm Uhr)* – with a stunning view thrown in for free.

② Asahi Beer Hall 🏢

Back on solid ground, **follow the canal to the banks of the Sumida River.** A great subject for a photo is the ② **Asahi Beer Hall** – or more precisely, the golden flame created by the designer Philippe Starck which, in a bizarre move, he placed on the roof of the building! Tokyoites have come up with an not-so-complimentary nickname for it: the golden turd. The headquarters of Asahi Brewery is more conventional – it's shaped like a giant beer mug.

Continue over the bridge to ❸ **Kaminarimon**, the main gate of the Asakusa Kannon Temple, easily recognisable by its giant red paper lantern. Before visiting the temple, take a rickshaw ride through the old entertainment district of ❹ **Asakusa → p. 32** – even if it's only for ten minutes! The friendly drivers speak good English. Afterwards, stroll through the quaint ❺ **Nakamise shopping street**. You can watch how traditional sweets such as deep-fried, filled dumplings are made – and then sample some.

12:00pm At the end of the shopping street, you will encounter another gate to the ❻ **Asakusa Kannon Temple → p. 33**. If you're lucky, a traditional festival may be taking place at this colourful temple. At the entrance, be sure to fan some of the smoke from the incense sticks toward yourself: it is said to stimulate hair growth! Inside the temple, you can find out what the future holds for you – take a small stick with a number from a wooden box and look in the corresponding drawer for a small note containing a fortune – with an English translation. **Walk past the Asakusa Shrine, cross through the Nitenmon Gate and follow the next major street on the right** to the ❼ **Matsuya department store**. On the lower level, you can buy bento boxes containing fish, meat, rice and vegetables for your lunch on the ferry. Departure time is 1pm!

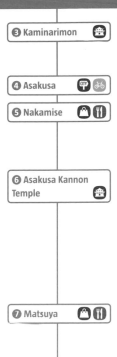

❸ Kaminarimon

❹ Asakusa

❺ Nakamise

❻ Asakusa Kannon Temple

❼ Matsuya

A great photo opportunity: The busy Nakamise shopping street!

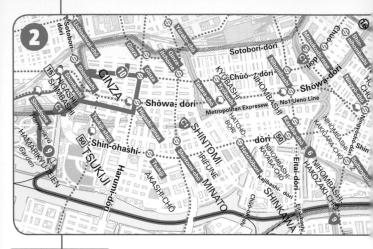

8 Tokyo Cruise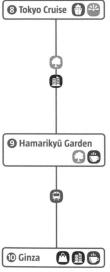

The ticket office for the **8 Tokyo Cruise** is located on the red Azuma Bridge. It's astonishing to see how green Tokyo looks from the water! In the spring, flowering pink cherry trees line the riverbanks and the promenade is adorned with flowers. Then the **Kokugikan Hall** appears on the left – the sumo wrestlers' arena. Two bridges further on, on the left, you can see a statue of Japan's most famous haiku poet, Bashō. Also on the left loom the towers of the **River City 21** residential district. Past the **Fish Market →** **p. 49**, on the right side, the ferry approaches its last stop, Hamarikyū. Stretch your legs in the **9 Hamarikyū-Garten** **→ p. 46**, and enjoy a bowl of matcha tea and sweets at the teahouse – with a spectacular view of the skyscrapers in **Shiodome. From the park, it's a ten-minute walk to the Shimbashi subway and suburban railway station.**

9 Hamarikyū Garden

10 Ginza

`03:30pm` North-east to Shimbashi lies Tokyo's most elegant shopping mile, **10 Ginza → p. 46**. Stroll along the central **Chuo-dori** and **Harumi-dori** as well as the side streets. **Ginza Natsuno** (Mon–Sat 10am–8pm, Sun 10am–7pm | 6-7-4 Ginza | Chūo-ku) offers an overwhelming selection of chopsticks – perfect small gifts! **Kyūkyodō** (Mon–Sat 10am–7:30pm, Sun 11am–7pm | 5-7-4 Ginza | Chūōku) specialises in paper products: exquisite *washi* paper, the most beautiful postcards and tasteful wrapping paper. Do you need a few more t-shirts? At the world's largest **Uni-qlo → p. 83** store, you can find very low-priced, good-quality functional clothing in many different colours. For a very

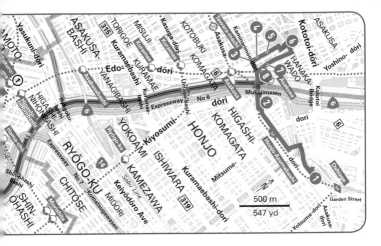

different price category, stop at **Mikimoto** → p. 83. Even if you're not interested in expensive pearls, the weird-looking, "holey" façade is worth a photo. At **Café Paulista** *(Mon–Sat 8:30am–9pm, Sun 11:30am–8pm | 8–9-1 Ginza | Chūo-ku)*, you can sink into a brown leather chair and look back on everything you've seen over a cup of coffee.

③ FUTURISTIC TOKYO

START: ❶ Shimbashi **END:** ❽ Ōedo Onsen Monogatari	1 day Walking time (without stops) 3 hours
Distance: 🚌 30 km/19 mi	

COSTS: Approx. ¥7700 per person for day pass on the suburban railway, admission tickets, tea and lunch breaks and Ferris wheel tickets

WHAT TO PACK: Bathing gear

What destination draws over 20 million visitors per year? Disneyland? No – Odaiba! The Tokyo Bay island is a sort of amusement park with a Ferris wheel, shopping centres, technology museum and a go-cart track. Have fun!

09:00am Starting at ❶ **Shimbashi** (A 10, G 08), buy a day ticket for the Yurikamome line. Your destination is **Odaiba** → p. 47, an artificially created island in the Bay of Tokyo.

❶ Shimbashi

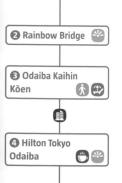

2 Rainbow Bridge

3 Odaiba Kaihin Kōen

4 Hilton Tokyo Odaiba

If you can secure a seat at the front window of your car, you're sure to get some INSIDER TIP great photos: as you approach the **2 Rainbow Bridge,** the driverless train makes an elegant loop onto the impressive suspension bridge.

Disembark at **3 Odaiba Kaihin Kōen and walk along the artificial sandy beach to Daiba Station.** Along the way, you're sure to catch sight of a futuristic building with a huge, shimmering silver ball. It looks like a giant screen – and no wonder: this is the headquarters of Fuji TV. You can sit in the café of the elegant **4 Hilton Tokyo Odaiba** and admire the skyscraper panorama in the Bay of Tokyo.

`12:30pm` **Follow the walkways to a wide promenade bet-ween Fuji TV and the Hotel Grand Nikko.** The ❺ **DiverCity Tokyo Plaza** shopping centre is perfect for a lunch break. **Akasaka Chibisuke** *(open daily 11am–11pm)*serves deli-cious *gyoza* – dumplings filled with meat, fish or vegeta-bles. Ready for another futuristic experience? Walk on to the ❻ **Miraikan** *(Wed–Mon 10am–5pm | Admission ¥620 | www.miraikan.jst.go.jp/en)*. The future has already arrived here, and you're invited to join the fun – with everything from space exploration to robotics.

`03:00pm` The present also offers plenty of excitement! For your next stop, **walk back** and dive into the shopping and amusement park ❼ **Palette Town**. It would be easy to spend several days here. Do you feel like going bowling or belting out some songs? Then head for **Tokyo Leisu-re Land**, a mixture of a gaming arcade, bowling alley and karaoke bar. Or would you rather get a bird's eye view of Odaiba? Then board the Ferris wheel – one of the world's highest at 115 m/377 ft. At the **Venus Fort**, an outlet mall decorated in Italian-style kitsch, you can wander through approximately 50 shops and a food court. Do you love cars? At `INSIDER TIP` **Megaweb**, a showroom for Toyota, Japan's top automobile manufacturer, you can race into the motorised future in a hybrid go-cart.

❺ DiverCity Tokyo Plaza

❻ Miraikan

❼ Palette Town

Elevated train and high-rises: The tour starts at Shimbashi

After so many lively visions of the future, it's time to take a relaxing journey into the peaceful past. **Ride one station back to the Telecom Center**. At **8**  INSIDER TIP **Ōedo Onsen Monogatari** *(open daily 11am–9am (yes, in the morning!) | Admission starting at ¥2480 | 2–57 Aomi | Kōtō-ku)*, a mixture of bath house and theme park, you can relax in traditional Japanese fashion in thermal spring water.

8 Ōedo Onsen Monogatari 🌀 ♨

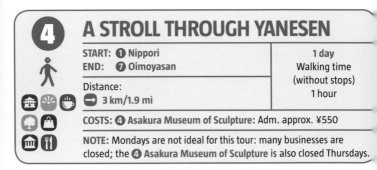

4 A STROLL THROUGH YANESEN

START: **1** Nippori END: **7** Oimoyasan	1 day Walking time (without stops) 1 hour
Distance: ➡ 3 km/1.9 mi	
COSTS: **4** Asakura Museum of Sculpture: Adm. approx. ¥550	
NOTE: Mondays are not ideal for this tour: many businesses are closed; the **4** Asakura Museum of Sculpture is also closed Thursdays.	

Clocks tick more slowly in Yanesen (Yanaka, Nezu and Sendagi). If you're seeking tranquillity or a have a sweet tooth, you can discover temples and shrines, arts and crafts shops, and perfect places to snack.

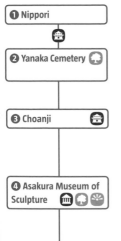

1 Nippori

2 Yanaka Cemetery 🌳

3 Choanji 🏯

4 Asakura Museum of Sculpture 🏛🌳♨

09:00am From the south exit of the suburban railway station **1** **Nippori, a path leads uphill on the left-hand side.** This takes you past the **Tennoji-Tempel**, with its beautiful Buddha statue, to the expansive **2** **Yanaka Cemetery**. When the cherry trees are in bloom in the springtime, this is a wonderful spot for *hanami* (cherry blossom viewing). Do you see some cats slinking around? This area is also known as "Cat City". **At the first large intersection inside the cemetery, the path on the right leads to** **3** **Choanji, in the middle of an old temple area.** With their traditional beams made of dark-coloured wood, the small temples radiate great tranquillity.

Now head to the right, toward the **4** **Asakura Museum of Sculpture → p. 48**. Here you get two insights at once: into the studio of a Japanese sculptor – containing lifelike sculptures of people and cats – and into a traditional Edo-period home. Plus, there's nature galore! Circle around the beautiful Zen water garden in the courtyard, and climb up to the roof garden, with its fantastic panoramic view.

`11:00am` Tokyo without shopping? Of course that will never do. **Follow the street to the next large fork; then continue diagonally to the right, past a shop full of cat-themed knick-knacks, then down the steps**. At the bottom is the beginning of the ❺ **Yanaka Ginza**, a traffic-free shopping street. Immediately on your right, you can purchase elegant bamboo and woven items at **Midoriya** *(open daily 11am–6pm)*. Have you ever sat on a lotus root? Small bamboo benches shaped like Japanese vegetables make an unusual gift. Another funny idea: a few metres further on the left side, you can order a `INSIDER TIP` personalised name stamp *(hanko)* at **Ito Manufacturing** with motifs such as kittens or pandas.

Now how about some street food for lunch – for example, pan-fried *mgenchi-katsu*, the Japanese take on croquettes. The **Kanekichien** tea and ceramic shop serves free green tea as a thank you for your visit. **Further down the street**, your sweet tooth will be delighted with the pretty **Waguriya** café *(Tue–Sun 11am–7pm)*. The delicious desserts featuring chestnuts vary according to the seasons; in the spring they include fresh strawberries.

`02:30pm` **Continue walking diagonally to the left, to the main street of Shinobazu Dori and follow it to the left. At the second set of traffic lights, turn right towards the** ❻ **Nezu Shrine** → p. 48, one of the most beautiful in Tokyo – with carp ponds, gingko trees and blooming azaleas in the springtime. **Walk back over a stone bridge to the main street. Before going to the Nezu subway station**, sweets lovers will want to make one last stop: the `INSIDER TIP` sweet potato desserts at ❼ **Oimoyasan** *(open daily 10am–7pm | 1–22-14 Nezu | Bunkyō-ku)* are out of this world.

❺ Yanaka Ginza

❻ Nezu Shrine

❼ Oimoyasan

TRAVEL WITH KIDS

As a precaution, you should put a note in your children's pockets stating the Japanese address and telephone number of your lodgings.

GHIBLI MUSEUM (ジブリ美術館)
(139 D2) (*∅ d2*)

Oscar-winner Hayao Miyazaki is the founding father of Japanese animated films (anime). At his museum in Inokashira Park, wild creatures and fantastical landscapes set the scene. Of course, you can also learn about how animated films are made. *Usually open Wed–Mon 10am–6pm (see website) | Admission according to age, ¥100–¥1000 (Tickets must be ordered in advance for a specific date; available as vouchers via post in Europe or in Japan at Lawson convenience stores) | 1–1–83 Shimorenjaku | 1–1–83 下連雀 | Mitaka-shi | 三鷹市 | www.ghibli-museum.jp/en | Suburban railway Chuo Line Mitaka*

INSIDER TIP HEIWA NO MORI KOEN (平和の森公園) (139 E3) (*∅ e3*)

In the "Peace Forest", children (and adults) can test their agility on obstacle courses with varying degrees of difficulty. You might get dirty and wet, but you will have loads of fun at a bargain price.

Bring snacks with you: only drinks are available for purchase in the park. *Tue–Sun 9:30am–4:30pm | Admission: adults ¥360, children ¥100 | 2–1 Heiwa no Mori Koen | 2–1 平和の森公園 | Ota-ku | 大田区 | Suburban railway Keikyu Heiwajima*

NATIONAL MUSEUM OF NATURE AND SCIENCE (国立科学博物館)
(133 D2) (*∅ P1*)

With exciting exhibitions ranging from dinosaurs to space travel, the whole family will get their money's worth. The 3D Theater 360 is particularly exciting; visitors of all ages get to stand on a bridge – and end up right in the film! *Tue–Sun 9am–5pm | Admission: adults ¥620, children and teens free | 7–20 Uenokoen | 7–20 上野公園 | Taito-ku | 台東区 | www.kahaku.go.jp | Subway G 16, H 17 Ueno | Yamanote loop line Ueno*

TAMA ZOO (多摩動物園)
(138 C3) (*∅ c3*)

You can easily spend a whole day at this zoo. With a total area of 523,000 m²/129 acres, animals from all over the world live mostly in spacious outdoor enclosures. *Thur–Tue 9:30am–5pm; closed 29 Dec–1 Jan | Admission ¥600, ages 13–15 ¥200, 12 and under free | 7–1–1 Hodokubo |*

There's a great variety of things for families to do – from the world's most-visited amusement park to the anime film museum

7-1-1 程久保 / *Hino-shi* / 日野市 / *www.to-kyo-zoo.net* / *Keiō Train (1 hour travel time from Shinjuku) Tamadōbutsukōenmae*

TOKYO DISNEY RESORT (東京ディズニーリゾート) (139 F3) (🕮 f3)

The two theme parks, Disneyland and DisneySea, are too much to cover in just one day. If you choose Disneyland, you can look forward to a break-neck ride through Big Thunder Mountain and a spectacular boat ride through Splash Mountain – or you can relax on a ride across Fantasyland. At the neighbouring DisneySea, the Indiana Jones ride or the free fall in the Tower of Terror attract a large number of visitors. Depending on the season, there are also special events. *Open daily 8am–10pm / Day pass: adults ¥7400, ages 12–17 ¥6400, ages 4–11 ¥4800 / 1–1 Maihama / 1–1 舞浜 / Urayasu-shi / 浦安市 / Chiba-ken / 千葉県 / www.tokyodisneyresort.jp/en / Suburban railway (Keiyō or Musashino from Tokyo Main Station) Maihama*

TOKYO SEA LIFE PARK (葛西臨海水族館) ★ (139 E3) (🕮 e3)

The ● *aquarium (Thur–Tue 9:30am–5pm; closed 29 Dec–1 Jan / Admission: adults ¥700, ages 13–15 ¥250, 12 and under free / www.tokyo-zoo.net/english/kasai/index.html)* under the giant glass dome at Tokyo Sea Life Park in Kasai Rinkai Park is one of the most beautiful in the world. The penguins are the main attraction! Afterwards, enjoy a walk in the adjoining *Bird Park (Open daily 9:15am–4:30pm / Free admission)* with freshwater and saltwater lakes. It's also fun to have a picnic in Tokyo's largest park or take a ride on the 🎡 *Ferris wheel (Mon–Fri 10am–8pm, Sat, Sun 10am–9pm / Admission: ages 3 and up ¥700)*. Kasai Rinkai Kōen / 6–2–3 Rinkaichō / 6–2–3 臨海町 / *Edogawa-ku* / 江戸川区 / *www.tokyo-zoo.net* / *Suburban railway (Keiyō Line from Tokyo Main Station) Kasai-rinkai-kōen or water bus from Takeshiba Pier*

FESTIVALS & EVENTS

Most of the festivals are Shinto in origin. People give thanks to the gods and celebrate with them at shrines and temples and in processions with portable shrines. And what would Tokyo be without its luxuriant cherry and plum blossoms in the spring? If a holiday falls on a Sunday, the following Monday is a non-working day.

FESTIVALS & EVENTS

JANUARY

Shortly before the turn of the year, bells in sacred places ring 108 times to drive out human desires – for example in Zōjōji (136 A4) (*ﾉﾉ M10*). In shrines and temples, people ask for the gods' blessings on the first days of the New Year – for example, at the Meiji Shrine (134 B2) (*ﾉﾉ E7–8*) and in Asakusa (133 F2) (*ﾉﾉ S1*).

2 Jan, 9:30am–3pm: the imperial family appears before the public at the Palace (132 A–B6) (*ﾉﾉ M6–7*).

FEBRUARY/MARCH

Plum blossom viewing from mid-February to early March at the Yushima-tenjin Shrine(1328 C3) (*ﾉﾉ O3*)

AnimeJapan: The world's largest anime fair at Tokyo Big Sight, late March (139 E3) (*ﾉﾉ e3*)

MARCH/APRIL

Sakura, the Time of the Cherry Blossoms: celebrated in parks and gardens – for example, at Shinjuku Gyoen (130 B–C6) (*ﾉﾉ F–G6*), in Ueno Park (132–129 C–D 1–2) (*ﾉﾉ P1–2*) or at the INSIDER TIP *Aoyama Cemetery* (135 D3) (*ﾉﾉ H9–10*)

APRIL/MAY

Spring Festival: Bunraku, Noh theatre and archery at the Meiji Shrine, late April– early May (134 B2) (*ﾉﾉ E7–8*)

Sanja-Matsuri: Procession in Asakusa with over 100 portable shrines on the 3rd weekend in May (133 F2) (*ﾉﾉ S1*)

JULY

Fireworks on the Sumida River, on the last Saturday of the month (133 F3–4) (*ﾉﾉ R3–4*)

AUGUST

INSIDER TIP *Yoshida no Himatsuri:* The official Mt. Fuji climbing season ends with this fire festival in Fujiyoshida (138 A3) (*ﾉﾉ a3*).

SEPTEMBER

Tsurugaoka Hachimangū Reitaisai in Kamakura. Portable shrine procession on the 15th; horseback archery on the 16th (139 D5) (*ﾉﾉ d5*)

Mostly cheerful: exuberant shrine festivals, sumptuous cherry blossoms in parks and gardens

OCTOBER/NOVEMBER

Ningyo-Kanshasai: On the first Sunday, a farewell ceremony is held at the Meiji Shrine for tens of thousands of dolls and cuddly toys, who have seen better days. (134 B2) (*ψ E7–8*).

Autumn Festival at the Meiji Shrine: Courtly dances and horseback archery, late October–early November (134 A–B1) (*ψ E7–8*)

Chrysanthemum Festival: Exhibition of the national flower in Shinjuku-Gyoen Park from late October to mid-November (130 B–C6) (*ψ F–G6*)

INSIDER TIP *Shichi-go-san:* Three and seven-year-old girls as well as three and five-year-old boys visit shrines in festive attire on 15 November – most photogenic at the Meiji Shrine (134 B2) (*ψ E7–8*).

INSIDER TIP *Design Festa:* Creative fireworks at the Tokyo Big Sight trade fair complex. At one of Asia's largest culture festivals in mid to late November, anyone may show of their creations. Also takes place in August (139 E3) (*ψ e3*)

Tokyo International Film Festival (TIFF): This prestigious festival takes place in Roppongi from late October to early November (135 E4) (*ψ J10*).

PUBLIC HOLIDAYS

1 Jan	New Year's Day
2nd Mon in Jan	Coming of Age Day
11 Feb	National Foundation Day
21 March	Spring Equinox Day
29 April	Shōwa Day
3 May	Constitution Memorial Day
4 May	Greenery Day
5 May	Children's Day
3rd Mon in July	Marine Day
11 Aug	Mountain Day
3rd Mon in Sept	Respect for the Aged Day
22/23 Sept	Autumnal Equinox Day
2nd Mon in Oct	Health-Sports Day
3 Nov	Culture Day
23 Nov	Labour Thanksgiving Day
23 Dec	Emperor's Birthday

LINKS, BLOGS, APPS & MORE

LINKS & BLOGS

www.bento.com With just a few clicks, you can find all kinds of restaurants, bars and cafés on this English-language website – in every city neighbourhood, for every budget. There's also information about Japanese culinary culture, recipes and background texts

www.embjapan.org This website provides lots of valuable information about the country and its people

www.japan-guide.com Current information in English – from Arrival to Zen classes. During cherry blossom season, there are scouts who keep you updated on which park has the most beautiful blossoms at any given time

www.gotokyo.org/en What's happening where, and how do I get there? Find answers to these questions on the City of Tokyo's official tourism website

https://tokyodesu.wordpress.com This blog is written by two foreigners living in Tokyo. Besides discussing current Japanese news stories, they provide travel guides to help you get the most out of your time (and money) in Tokyo

http://wandertokyo.com Travel information, cultural facts, and good tips on living and food in Japan. You can find advice, recommendations and information for foreigners working and studying in Japan (particularly Tokyo) that are not always easy to find in English

www.japanvisitor.blogspot.com Well structured, regularly updated English-language blog with lots of information about Japan with photos and travel tips

www.facebook.com/TokyoFanClub By Tokyo fans for future Tokyo fans

Regardless of whether you are still researching your trip or already in Tokyo: these addresses will provide you with more information, videos and networks to make your holiday even more enjoyable.

www.tokyogaijins.com Join *gaijins* (foreigners) living in Tokyo for a hike up Mt. Fuji or a boat tour

www.facebook.com/tokyocycling For anyone who doesn't like packed subways and long walks, but prefers to hop on a bike

https://www.dailymotion.com/video/x12ww8o UK documentary about the world's busiest train station – Shinjuku

VIDEOS & MUSIC

metropolis.co.jp/podcast Professional podcast from the English-language city magazine Metropolis about cultural subjects in Tokyo

www.interfm.co.jp InterFM 89.7 Mhz is currently the only radio station in Tokyo that broadcasts in English. In case of a disaster such as an earthquake, you can find clear information here

https://www.youtube.com/watch?v=IsngamFa1ps A friendly American gives practical tips on "How to survive your first hour in Japan (but really Tokyo)"

APPS

Tokyo Map and Walks A practical guide with walking tours to some of Tokyo's most important attractions

Tokyo Location Guide Tokyo is a popular backdrop – for example, in music videos like The Killers' "Read My Mind" or films like "Lost in Translation". With this app, you can find the famous locations

Tokyo Handy Guide You'll never get lost in Tokyo with this English-language app. It's also available offline

Tokyo Subway Navigation You'll undoubtedly use the subways and suburban railway to get from A to B in Tokyo, so good to have a station map in your smartphone

TRAVEL TIPS

Direct flights from London to Tokyo start at around £700 and take 11-12 hours. SAS *(www.flysas.com)* and Lufthansa *(www.lufthansa.com)* offer somewhat cheaper flights with one stopover; the trip then takes approx. 17 hours. Direct from New York to Tokyo costs about $1,800 and takes about 14 hours. ANA *(www.ana.co.jp/en/us)* and Air China *(www.airchina.com.cn/en)* offer flights with one stopover for significantly less; travel time is 20-25 hours. Japan Airlines *(www.jal.co.jp/yokosojapan)* and All Nippon Airways *(www.ana.co.jp)* may also offer special prices to tourists booking from Europe. Also check offers from discount airlines like JetStar *(www.jetstar.com)*,

RESPONSIBLE TRAVEL

While travelling, you can also make a big impact. Keep your carbon footprint in mind for your travel to and from Tokyo *(www.atmosfair.de/en; myclimate.org)* – for example, by planning your route in an environmentally friendly manner *(www.routerank.com)* – but also respect the nature and culture of your destination country *(www.sustainabletravel.org; www.destinet.eu)*. Particularly as a tourist, it's important to pay attention to aspects such as protecting the environment *(www.wwf.org)*, using regional products, driving less, saving water and much more. If you want to learn more about ecotourism, see *www.ecotourism.org, www.greenglobaltravel.com.*

Peach *(www.flypeach.com)* or Skymark *(www.skymark.co.jp)* – the earlier you book, the better.

Narita International Airport is located approx. 60 km/37 mi east of the city centre. Taxis cost approx. £185/$250. Orange busses operated by *Airport Limousine (approx. £22/$30 | Subway station Z 10 Suitengumae)* stop at Tokyo City Air Terminal (T-CAT) and major hotels; the trip takes about 70 minutes. Keisei busses cost approx. *£6/$8 (www.keiseibus.co.jp | Suburban railway M 17 Tokyo)*; the drive to Tokyo's main station takes a little over an hour.

Narita Express (NEX): The airport express train operated by Japan Railways goes to Tokyo Main Station *(approx. £20/$25)* with further stops in Shinjuku, Ikebukuro, Shibuya and Yokohama. All seats are reserved. Japan Rail Pass holders *(www.japanrailpass.net)* can use the NEX.

Skyliner: This private express train reaches Nippori in just 36 minutes *(approx. £15/$20)* and Ueno a few minutes later. Continue on by suburban rail or subway: a good solution if you're travelling light. The fast trains on the Keisei line *(approx. 75 min | approx. £6/$8)* are cheaper, but not as fast as the Skyliner.

Domestic flights – and increasingly, international ones – land at Haneda Airport outside of Tokyo *(www.hanedatokyo-access.com)*. From here, you take the *monorail* to Hamamatsucho and connect to the Yamanote Line for all of the major stations. Taxis to the city centre cost between £45/$60 and £70/$95. Be sure to take into account the possibility of traffic jams on the road to and from Haneda.

The three Shinkansen bullet train lines all end at Tokyo Main Station. The ter-

From arrival to weather

Your holiday from start to finish: the most important addresses and information for your trip to Tokyo.

minus station for other trains coming from the north is Ueno; from the west it's Shinjuku; all others end at Tokyo Main Station. Connections to subways and suburban railway are available at all stations.

BANKS & CURRENCY EXCHANGE

Japan is a cash country – particularly outside the city, but also in smaller shops and restaurants in Tokyo. It's best to exchange large amounts of cash when you arrive at the airport. In banks *(Mon–Fri 9am–3pm)*, the process is time-consuming. Bring a credit card with a PIN for withdrawing cash from ATMs; you can then use the cash machines at the post office or 7-Eleven convenience stores. Note: Maestro cards do not work in Japan.

CITY TOURS

FREE GUIDED TOURS FOR FOREIGN TOURISTS

Volunteer guides at City Hall in Shinjuku offer ten informative guided tours for small groups. The guides work as volunteers; you only need to pay for admission tickets and transportation. *http://www.tokyofreeguide.org/*

SKYBUS TOKYO

An open double-decker bus: four routes with explanations in several languages. *http://skybus.jp/*

CLIMATE & TRAVEL SEASONS

Attractive times to visit are spring, when the cherry blossoms emerge (March/April) and autumn (November), when

CURRENCY CONVERTER

£	JPY	JPY	£
1	150	100	0.66
5	752	200	1.33
10	1,505	500	3.32
20	3,010	800	5.31
30	4,514	1000	6.64
50	7,524	3000	19.92
80	12,039	5000	33.20
90	13,543	7000	46.48
100	15,048	9000	59.76

$	JPY	JPY	$
1	107	100	0.93
5	537	200	1.86
10	1,073	500	4.66
20	2,147	800	7.45
30	3,220	1000	9.31
50	5,366	3000	27.93
80	8,586	5000	46.55
90	9,659	7000	65.17
100	10,733	9000	83.97

For current exchange rates see www.xe.com

maple and gingko trees are bursting with colour. Avoid July and August, when the heat and humidity are unbearable. The winter months are often mild and sunny until well into December. January/February bring more rain with temperatures below 10 °C/50 °F.

The official weather service *(www.jma.go.jp/en/yoho)* provides information about storm warnings, tsunamis and seismic activity.

COMMUNICATION

First the good news: In Tokyo, signs at railway stations and on public transport are in both Japanese characters and Latin letters. In most trains, announcements are in Japanese and English. Now the somewhat less good news: Even in the capital, very few natives speak English. This makes some Japanese people so uncomfortable that they will walk past you without a word if you ask them for an address. Normally, however, people are friendly and helpful when dealing with foreigners – even helping to find a Japanese person who speaks English.

CUSTOMS

All travellers must fill out customs declarations (forms are distributed on the aircraft). In addition to normal luggage, you may bring either 400 cigarettes, 100 cigars or 500 g (17.6 oz) of tobacco as well as 60 ml of perfume. Travellers over 18 years old may bring three bottles of spirits or alcoholic beverages (2.28 l/2.4 qt). You may also bring in items duty free if their value on the foreign market is less than ¥200,000 (approx. £1270/$1700).

Upon returning to the UK, travellers from non-EU counties are allowed to enter with the following tax-free amounts: 200 cigarettes or 100 cigarillos or 50 cigars or 250g smoking tobacco; 2 l wine and spirts with less than 22 percent alcohol; 1 l spirits with over 22 percent vol alcohol. *www.gov.uk/duty-free-goods*
Travellers to the United States who are returning residents of the country do not have to pay duty on articles purchased overseas up to the value of 800 US$, but there are limits on the amount of alcoholic beverages and tobacco products. For international travel regulations for US residents, please see *www.cbp.gov*.

DIPLOMATIC MISSIONS

BRITISH EMBASSY (135 D5) (*ω J11*)
No 1 Ichiban-cho, Chiyoda-ku | Tel. 52 11 11 00 | Subway Hanzomon

US EMBASSY (135 E4) (*ω K11*)
1-10-5 Akasaka Minato-ku, Tokyo | Tel. 32 24 50 00 | Subway Toranomon

ELECTRICITY

Currents in Japan are only 100 V. Power supply units for most mobile phones, laptops and cameras are designed for between 100 and 240 V, but be sure to double check before connecting your device. You will also need an adapter for flat-pin sockets. Note: If you buy an electronic device in Japan, be sure it can tolerate the normal voltage in your home country!

EMERGENCY

Police (Tel. 1 10); Ambulance and fire department (Tel. 1 19); instructions on what to do in an earthquake: www.metro.tokyo.jp/ENGLISH/GUIDE/BOSAI/index.htm

ENTRY

You will need a valid passport; when you arrive, you will receive a permit to stay for three months.

EVENT CALENDAR

Available in free city magazines like *Metropolis* or *Time Out*; concert schedules at *www.tokyogigguide.com*.

HEALTH

Medical care in Tokyo is good, but expensive. There are doctors' offices, small clinics, drugstores and chemists' in every neighbourhood but language can sometimes be a problem. As a precaution, you should always keep the number for the *Tokyo Medical Information Center (Mon–Fri 9am–8pm | Tel. 52 85 81 81)* within reach; it can give you information (in English) about hospitals and specialist physicians. You can obtain a list of English-speaking doctors and hospitals from the Tourist Information Center. If you need prescription, it's best to bring it from home.

INFORMATION BEFORE YOU GO

JAPAN NATIONAL TOURISM ORGANIZATION (JNTO)

Provides brochures, including information on the economical Welcome Inns (WI). *Queensway, 3rd floor, 32, London, UK | Telw +44 20 7398 5670; One Grand Central Place, 60 East 42nd Street, Suite 448, New York, NY 10165, USA | Tel. +1 213 623-1952 www.jnto.go.jp*

INFORMATION IN TOKYO

TOKYO TOURIST INFORMATION CENTER (130 A5) (*∅ E5*)

The centre for the city of Tokyo at City Hall (other branches at Haneda Airport and Keisei Ueno Station) provides advice, brochures and maps. *No 1 Bldg. | 2–8-1 Nishi-Shinjuku | Shinjuku-ku | Tel. 03 53 21 30 77 | Subway E 28 Tochōmae*

TOURIST INFORMATION CENTER (NARITA AIRPORT) (0) (*∅ 0*)

Information centres are located in both terminals of Narita Airport.

TOURIST INFORMATION CENTER (TIC) (136 B1) (*∅ O8*)

Offers various brochures, city and subway maps and assistance with further travel within Japan. The centre can also connect you with tourist guides and has a Welcome Inn service. Always keep the TIC phone number at hand. *Shin Tokyo Bldg. | 3–3-1 Marunouchi | Chiyoda-ku | Tel. 03 32 01 33 31 | Subway H 07, C 09 Hibiya | Yamanote loop line Yūrakuchō*

INTERNET & WIFI

Unfortunately, Tokyo does not have a comprehensive Wi-Fi network. Some restaurants, hotels, and most central stations of the Tokyo subway (Metro) offer free Wi-Fi connections (for example, *Wired Cafe Shibuya QFront (134 B4) (∅ E10) (Open daily | 6F QFront |Udagawachō 21–6 | Shibuya-ku)*. A list of free Wi-Fi hotspots is available at *www.freespot.com/users/map_e. html*. NTT Communications offers tourists two weeks of free access to their hotspots *(flets.com/freewifi/service.html)*. Or rent a mobile Wi-Fi router at the airport – for example, at Softbank *(www.*

ADRESSES

The majority of the streets in Tokyo have no names. The addresses read like a secret code – for example: "2–23-1 Okamoto, Setagaya-ku". What this means is: go to the municipality of Setagaya; in the district of Okamoto, in the second sub-district, look in the 23rd house block for house number 1. Unfortunately, this is just as complicated as it sounds. An area map is helpful; otherwise, you can find help at any of the many police stations *(kōban)*.

softbank-rental.jp/en). The provider Pupuru *(www.pupuru.com/en/service/emobile)* will send a mobile Wi-Fi router to you at the airport or your lodgings. Another alternative is a data SIM card for your mobile phone – for example, Japan Travel SIM *(https://t.iijmio.jp/en).* Free Wi-Fi is available at airports.

PHONE & MOBILE PHONE

Public telephones often only accept phone cards. The basic price for a local call is ¥10; overseas calls are only available at phones marked "International Call". Phone cards *(telefon-kado)* with ¥1000 credit are available from machines or at hotels and railway station kiosks. Prepaid cards *(puripaido-kado)* are recommended for international calls. These are available at convenience stores such as Lawson or 7-Eleven. A one-minute call to the UK during working hours costs approx. £2; to the US $2.50.

Country codes for UK: +44; USA/Canada +1; Tokyo from other countries: +813. For landline calls and calls using phone cards: network provider's prefix + 010 + country code. Landline calls to Tokyo from inside Japan begin with 03.

Only UMTS-capable cell phones work in Japan. Your network operator must be a contracting partner with NTT II, DoCoMo or Softbank Mobile. You can hire a mobile phone or SIM card at the airport. You can find out about this before you travel – for example, at Softbank *(www.softbank-rental.jp/en).* The Renta Fone Japan company *(www.rentafonejapan.com)* will send your rental phone to your lodgings. Be sure to clarify activation terms for international calls!

WEATHER IN TOKYO

	Jan	Feb	March	April	May	June	July	Aug	Sept	Okt	Nov	Dec
Daytime temperatures in °C/°F	9/48	9/48	12/54	18/64	22/72	25/77	29/84	30/86	27/81	20/68	16/61	11/52
Nighttime temperatures in °C/°F	-1/30	-1/30	3/37	4/39	13/55	19/66	22/72	23/73	19/66	13/55	7/45	1/34
☀	6	6	6	6	6	5	6	7	4	4	5	5
☂	6	7	10	11	12	12	11	10	13	12	8	5

POST

Postcards to Europe or the United States cost ¥70; airmail letters up to 20 g/0.88 oz cost ¥110.

PRICES & CURRENCY

Tokyo ranks among the most expensive cities in the world. Caution: The exchange rate between the Yen and other currencies fluctuates wildly!

PUBLIC TRANSPORT

Public transport is out of service between approx. 1am and 5am. There are private and public suburban railway and subway lines; each has its own ticket counters and gates. Note: if you transfer from the subway (Metro, Toei) to the suburban railway (JR), the cost is higher than if you tranfer within a single system.

To avoid constantly buying new tickets when you switch trains, purchase a Suica or Pasmo card from a machine or ticket counter (¥2000 incl. deposit). With these rechargeable plastic cards, you can pay for your bus or subway ride simply by placing the card on the scanner – you can also use them to shop at convenience stores. If you have too little the credit for a fare, pay the difference at your destination at a "Fare Adjustment' machine. If you prefer to buy individual paper tickets and are unsure of how much you need to pay, simply choose the least expensive ticket and pay the difference at your destination. Note: On many lines there are also express trains, which do not stop at every station (shown in red on the display panel). One more tip: Bus travel is difficult if you don't understand Japanese.

BUDGETING

Coffee	starting at £1.75/$2.45 *for one cup*
Souvenir/gift	approx. £7/$10 *for a pair of chopsticks*
Subway	approx. £8/$11 *for a day pass*
Noodle soup	approx. £3/$4.30 *at a stand-up snack bar*
Sushi	about £0.90/$1.25 *for 2 pieces on a conveyor belt*
Cinema	approx. £13/$18.50 *for one ticket*

TAXI

There are plenty of taxis, but they're expensive. The starting price for the first 2 km (1.25 mi) is ¥730 (approx. £5/$7. A 20 percent surcharge is added between 10pm and 5am. However, the cars are sparkling clean, drivers wear white gloves and the rear doors open and close automatically (please don't slam them from the outside!). You can hail a taxi anywhere: a red light behind the windscreen indicates that a taxi is empty; green or no light means it's occupied.

TIME

Japan is seven hours behind the UK; six hours behind during European summer time. It's 14 hours behind the US East Coast, 17 hours behind the West Coast (daylight savings time: 13 and 16 hours, respectively). Japan does observe daylight savings time.

TIPPING

There is no tipping in Japan!

USEFUL PHRASES JAPANESE

PRONOUNCIATION

As an aid to pronunciation, the following phonetic spellings have been used:

"a"   for a short open vowel as in "butter"
"e"   for a short vowel as in "pen"
"i"   for a short vowel as in "fin"
„o"   for a short open vowel as in "lock"
"u"   for a short open vowel as in "foot"
"ō", "ū" indicate an elongation of the vowel as in "port", "clue"
"ai"   for a diphthong as in "hi"
"r"   is not rolled, but is actually a combination of "r" und "l"

Double consonants (as in "chotto", "shuppatsu") have a short breath between the consonants (chotto roughly chot-!-to, shuppatsu roughly shup-!-patsu)

IN BRIEF	
Yes./No./Maybe.	はい／いいえ／たぶん [Hai./Iiye./Tabun.]
Please./Thank you.	どうぞ／ありがとう [Dōzo./Arigatō.]
Excuse me!	すみません [Sumimasen!]
May I ...?	...してもいいですか [... shtemo ii deska?]
What did you say?	すみません。もう一度お願いします [Sumimasen. Mō ichido onegai shimas.]
Do you have...?	...はありますか [... wa arimas ka?]
How much does ... cost?	...はいくらですか [... wa ikura deska?]
I like (don't like) this.	...は気に入りました（入りません） [... wa ki ni irimashita (irimasen).]
good/bad	良い／悪い [yoi/warui]
broken/doesn't work	壊れています [kowarete imas]
Help!/Attention!/Watch out!	助けて／気をつけて／気をつけて [Taskete!/Ki o tskete!/Ki o tskete!]
Ambulance	救急車 [kyūkyūsha]
Police/Fire department	警察／消防 [keisatsu/shōbō]

GREETINGS & PARTINGS	
Good morning!/afternoon!	おはようございます／こんにちは [Ohayō gozaimas!/Konnichi-wa!]
Good evening!/night!	こんばんは／お休みなさい [Komban-wa!/Oyasuminasai!]

日本語が話せますか。

'Do you speak Japanese?' This guide will help you to say the basic words and phrases in Japanese.

Hello!/Good-bye!	こんにちは/さようなら	[Konnichi-wa!/Sayōnara!]
Bye-bye/See you later!	それじゃ、またね	[Sore ja mata ne!]
My name is ...	...と申します	[... to mōshimas.]
What is your name?	お名前を教えてください	
(formal)	[Onama-e o oshiete kudasai?]	
(informal)	名前は何ですか	[Nama-e wa nan deska?]
I come from ...	...から来ました	[... kara kimashta.]

DATE & TIME

Monday/Tuesday	月曜日/火曜日	[getsu-yōbi/ka-yōbi]
Wednesday/Thursday	水曜日/木曜日	[sui-yōbi/moku-yōbi]
Friday/Saturday	金曜日/土曜日	[kin-yōbi/do-yōbi]
Sunday/weekday	日曜日/平日	[nichi-yōbi/hei-jitsu]
holiday	祝日	[shuku-jitsu]
today/tomorrow/yesterday	今日/明日/昨日	[kyō/ashta/kinō]
hour/minute	時間/分	[jikan/fun]
day/night/week	昼間/夜中 週間	[hiruma/yonaka/shūkan]
month/year	月/年	[getsu (gatsu)/nen]
What time is it?	今何時ですか	[Ima nan-ji deska?]
It's three o'clock.	三時です	[San-ji des.]
It's three thirty.	三時半です	[San-ji-han des.]

TRAVEL

open/closed	開いています/閉まっています	
	[aite imas/shimatte imas]	
Entrance/Exit	入り口/出口	[iriguchi/deguchi]
Departure/Arrival	出発/到着	[shuppatsu/tōchakku]
Toilets/Ladies/Men	お手洗い/女(性)/男(性)	[ote-arai/josei/dansei]
Where is...?/Where are...?	...はどこですか	[... wa doko deska?]
right/left	右/左	[migi/hidari]
straight ahead/back	まっすぐ/戻る	[massugu/modoru]
near/far	近い/遠い	[chikai/tō-i]
subway/taxi	地下鉄/タクシー	[chikatetsu/takshii]
bus (subway) stop/taxi stand	停/タクシー乗り場	[tei/takshii-noriba]
city map/road map	地図	[chizu]
station/port	駅/港	[eki/minato]
airport	空港	[kūkō]
timetable/ticket	時刻表/切符	[jikokuhyō/kippu]
one-way/round trip	片道/往復	[katamichi/ōfuku]
train/platform	電車/番線	[densha/ban-sen]

FOOD & DRINK

We would like to reserve a table for four people for this evening.	今夜の四人分の席を予約したいのですが [Konya no yonin-bun no seki o yoyaku shtai no des ga.]
The menu, please.	メニューをお願いします [Menyū o onegai shimas.]
May I have ...?	... を頂いてもいいですか [... o itadaite mo ii des ka?]
salt/pepper/sugar	塩/こしょう/砂糖 [shio/koshō/satō]
I would like to pay, please.	お勘定お願いします [O-kanjō onegai shimas.]
bill/receipt	お勘定/領収書 [o-kanjō/ryōshūsho]

SHOPPING

Where can I find ...?	... はどこにありますか [... wa doko ni arimas ka?]
I'm looking for ...	... を探しています [... o sagashte imas.]
chemist (pharmacy)/drugstore	薬局/ドラッグストア [yakkyoku/doraggu-stoa]
bakery/market	パン屋/市場 [pan-ya/ichiba]
shopping centre/department store	ショッピングセンター/デパート [shopping sentaa/depōto]
supermarket	スーパー [sūpaa]
expensive/cheap/price	高い/安い/値段 [takai/yasui/nedan]

ACCOMODATION

I have a room reserved.	部屋を予約したのですが [Heya o yoyaku shta no desga.]
Do you still have ...?	... はまだありますか [... wa mada arimas ka?]
single room	シングルルーム [shinguru rūm]
double room	ダブルルーム [daburu rūm]
breakfast/half board/full board	朝食付き/二食付き/三食付 [chōshoku-tski/ni-shoku-tski/san-shoku-tski]
shower/bath	シャワー/お風呂 [shawaa/o-furo]
key/key card	鍵/カードキー [kagi/kaado-kee]
luggage/suitcase/bag	荷物/スーツケース/かばん [nimotsu/sūtskes/kaban]

BANKS, MONEY & CREDIT CARDS

bank/ATM	銀行/ＡＴＭ [ginkō/Ey-Tee-Em]
I would like to exchange ... pounds (dollars).	... ポンド(ドル)を両替したいのですが [... pondo (doru) o ryōga-e shtai no des ga.]
cash/EC card/credit card	現金/ヨーロッパのキャッシュカード/クレジットカード [genkin/yōroppa no kyasshu-kaado/kurejitto-kaado]

HEALTH

doctor/dentist/paediatrician	医者/歯医者/小児科 [isha/ha-isha/shōnika]
hospital/emergency room	病院/当番医 [byō-in/tōban-i]
fever/pain	熱/痛み [netsu/itami]
diarrhoea/nausea	下痢/吐き気 [geri/haki-ke]
infected/injured	炎症があります/怪我をしました [enshō ga arimas/kega o shimashta]
plaster (band-aid)/bandage/painkiller/tablet	ばんそうこう/包帯/痛み止め/錠剤 [bansōkō/hōtai/itami-dome/jōzai]

TELECOMMUNICATIONS & MEDIA

stamp/letter	切手/手紙 [kitte/tegami]
postcard	葉書 [hagaki]
I need a phone card for landline calls.	固定電話用のテレフォンカードを下さい。 [Kotei-denwa yō no telefon-kaado o kudasai.]
I'm looking for a prepaid card for my mobile phone.	携帯電話用のプリペイドカードを探しています [Keitai-denwa yō no puri-peido kaado o sagashte imas.]
outlet/adapter/charging unit	コンセント/アダプター/充電器 [konsento/adaputaa/jūdenki]
computer/battery/rechargeable battery	コンピュータ/電池/充電池 [kompyūta/denchi/jūdenchi]
Internet connection/Wi-Fi	インターネット接続/無線LAN [intaanetto-setsuzoku/musen-laan]
e-mail/file/print	メール/ファイル/を印刷する [meelu/fairu/o insatsu suru]

NUMBERS

0	ゼロ [zero]		15	十五 [jū-go]
1	一 [ichi]		16	十六 [jū-roku]
2	二 [ni]		17	十七 [jū-shichi/jū-nana]
3	三 [san]		18	十八 [jū-hachi]
4	四 [shi, yon]		19	十九 [jū-kyū/jū-ku]
5	五 [go]		70	七十 [nana-jū]
6	六 [roku]		80	八十 [hachi-jū]
7	七 [shichi, nana]		90	九十 [kyū-jū]
8	八 [hachi]		100	百 [hyaku]
9	九 [kyū, ku]		200	二百 [ni-hyaku]
10	十 [jū]		1000	千 [sen]
11	十一 [jū-ichi]		2000	二千 [ni-sen]
12	十二 [jū-ni]		10000	一万 [ichi-man]
13	十三 [jū-san]		1/2	二分の一 [ni-bun no ichi]
14	十四 [jū-yon]		1/4	四分の一 [yon-bun no ichi]

STREET ATLAS

The green line indicates the Discovery Tour "Tokyo at a glance"
The blue line indicates the other Discovery Tours
All tours are also marked on the pull-out map

Photo: Cherry blossoms along the moat at the Imperial Palace

Exploring Tokyo

The map on the back cover shows how
the area has been sub-divided.

KEY TO STREET ATLAS

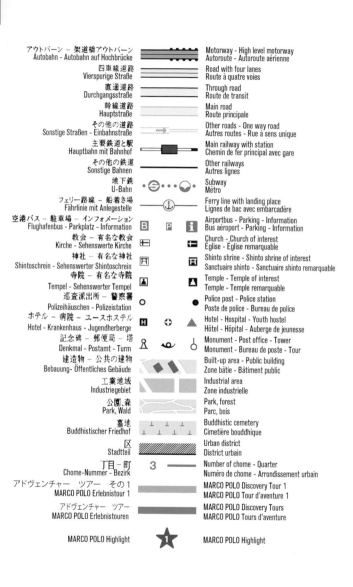

アウトバーン – 架道橋アウトバーン Autobahn - Autobahn auf Hochbrücke		Motorway - High level motorway Autoroute - Autoroute aérienne
四車線道路 Vierspurige Straße		Road with four lanes Route à quatre voies
直通道路 Durchgangsstraße		Through road Route de transit
幹線道路 Hauptstraße		Main road Route principale
その他の道路 Sonstige Straßen - Einbahnstraße		Other roads - One way road Autres routes - Rue à sens unique
主要鉄道と駅 Hauptbahn mit Bahnhof		Main railway with station Chemin de fer principal avec gare
その他の鉄道 Sonstige Bahnen		Other railways Autres lignes
地下鉄 U-Bahn		Subway Métro
フェリー路線 – 船着き場 Fährlinie mit Anlegestelle		Ferry line with landing place Lignes de bac avec embarcadère
空港バス – 駐車場 – インフォメーション Flughafenbus - Parkplatz - Information		Airportbus - Parking - Information Bus aéroport - Parking - Information
教会 – 有名な教会 Kirche - Sehenswerte Kirche		Church - Church of interest Eglise - Eglise remarquable
神社 – 有名な神社 Shintoschrein - Sehenswerter Shintoschrein		Shinto shrine - Shinto shrine of interest Sanctuaire shinto - Sanctuaire shinto remarquable
寺院 – 有名な寺院 Tempel - Sehenswerter Tempel		Temple - Temple of interest Temple - Temple remarquable
巡査派出所 – 警察署 Polizeihäuschen - Polizeistation		Police post - Police station Poste de police - Bureau de police
ホテル – 病院 – ユースホステル Hotel - Krankenhaus - Jugendherberge		Hotel - Hospital - Youth hostel Hôtel - Hôpital - Auberge de jeunesse
記念碑 – 郵便局 – 塔 Denkmal - Postamt - Turm		Monument - Post office - Tower Monument - Bureau de poste - Tour
建造物 – 公共の建物 Bebauung- Öffentliches Gebäude		Built-up area - Public building Zone bâtie - Bâtiment public
工業地域 Industriegebiet		Industrial area Zone industrielle
公園、森 Park, Wald		Park, forest Parc, bois
墓地 Buddhistischer Friedhof		Buddhistic cemetery Cimetière bouddhique
区 Stadtteil		Urban district District urbain
丁目 – 町 Chome-Nummer - Bezirk	3	Number of chome - Quarter Numéro de chome - Arrondissement urbain
アドヴェンチャー ツアー その1 MARCO POLO Erlebnistour 1		MARCO POLO Discovery Tour 1 MARCO POLO Tour d'aventure 1
アドヴェンチャー ツアー MARCO POLO Erlebnistouren		MARCO POLO Discovery Tours MARCO POLO Tours d'aventure
MARCO POLO Highlight	⭐1	MARCO POLO Highlight

MARCO POLO TRAVEL GUIDES

Travel with
Insider
Tips

INDEX

This index lists all the sights and destinations mentioned in this guide, as well as some important streets, names and terms. Page numbers shown in bold indicate the main entry.

WRITE TO US

e-mail: info@marcopologuides.co.uk

Did you have a great holiday?
Is there something on your mind?
Whatever it is, let us know!
Whether you want to praise, alert us
to errors or give us a personal tip –
MARCO POLO would be pleased to
hear from you.
We do everything we can to provide the
very latest information for your trip.

Nevertheless, despite all of our authors'
thorough research, errors can creep in.
MARCO POLO does not accept any
liability for this. Please contact us by
e-mail or post.
MARCO POLO Travel Publishing Ltd
Pinewood, Chineham Business Park
Crockford Lane, Chineham
Basingstoke, Hampshire RG24 8AL
United Kingdom

PICTURE CREDITS
On the cover: Tokyo, Shinjuku (Laif/GAMMA-RAPHO: J. F. Raga)
Photos: DuMont Bildarchiv: Hackenberg (62); Gettyimages/praetorianphoto (3); Glow Images/amanaimages:
Doable (68 left); Laif: Grandadam (6), Gumm (69), G. Hohenberg (22), Kirchgessner (39, 92/93), M. Kirchgess-
ner (99, 109), J. Souteyrat (73, 94), J. Whitlow Delano (67), Zuder (41); Laif/Arcaid: P. Bond (43); Laif/GAMMA-
RAPHO: K. Kasahara (114), J. F. Raga (1 top, 128/129); Laif/hemis.fr (112), C. Moirenc (50/51, 116 top), Frilet (10),
Maisant (68 right), Left Maisant (36), D. Zylberyng (5, 12/13, 100/101); Laif/le Figaro Magazine: Lefranc (89);
Laif/Polaris: Hockstein (11), D. Lefranc (70, 116 below); Laif/REA: Decout (81), J. Leynse (83); Laif/robertharding:
S. Black (47), Godong (4 below, 60/61); Laif/Zenit: Boening (84/85, 97); Look: A. Schwab (32/33, 65, 74/75);
Look/age fotostock (2, 7, 26/27, 54); mauritius images: P. Kaczynski (18 below), J. F. Raga (17, 20/21), Vidler
(Klappe right, 14/15, 115), S. Vidler (76); mauritius images/ Prisma by Dukas Presseagentur/Alamy (34); mauri-
tius images/China Span/Alamy: K. Su (25); mauritius images/age fotostock. J. F. Raga (56); mauritius Images/
Alamy (90/91, 113), T. Bognar (44), E. Katsumata (49, 117), S. Nogueira (78), A. Segre (18 M.); mauritius ima-
ges/Author's Image (59); mauritius images/Diversion: T. Miyamoto (53); mauritius images/EDU Vision/Alamy
(18 top); mauritius images/FantasticJapan/Alamy (19 top); mauritius images/Hemis.fr. D. Zylberyng (Klappe
left); mauritius images/J Marshall -Tribaleye Images/Alamy (86); mauritius images/John Warburton-Lee: S. Po-
liti Markovina (4 top, 30), mauritius images/John Warburton-Lee/Travel Pix Collection (8); mauritius images/
Westend61: H. Loebermann (105); mauritius images/World Discovery/Alamy (19 below); H. Pohling (9)

1st edition 2019
Worldwide Distribution: Marco Polo Travel Publishing Ltd, Pinewood, Chineham Business Park,
Crockford Lane, Basingstoke, Hampshire RG24 8AL, United Kingdom. Email: sales@marcopolouk.com
© MAIRDUMONT GmbH & Co. KG, Ostfildern
Chief editor: Marion Zorn
Author: Hans-Günther Krauth; Co-author: Sonja Blaschke; Editor: Karin Liebe
Programme supervision: Lucas Forst-Gill, Susanne Heimburger, Johanna Jiranek, Nikolai Michaelis, Martin Silber-
mann, Kristin Wittemann, Tim Wohlbold
Picture editor: Stefanie Wiese, Gabriele Forst
What's hot: wunder media, Munich
Cartography street atlas: © MAIRDUMONT, Ostfildern; Cartography pull-out map: © MAIRDUMONT, Ostfildern
Design cover, p. 1, pull-out map cover: Karl Anders – Büro für Visual Stories, Hamburg; design inside:
milchhof:atelier, Berlin; design Discovery Tours, p. 2/3: Susan Chaaban Dipl.-Des. (FH)
Translated from German by Mary Dobrian, Cologne
Editorial office: trans texas publishing services GmbH, Cologne; Dorothy Schaps, Cologne
Prepress: trans texas publishing services GmbH, Cologne
Phrase book in cooperation with Ernst Klett Sprachen GmbH, Stuttgart,
editorial by PONS Wörterbücher

MIX
Paper from
responsible sources
FSC® C124385

DOS AND DON'TS 👆

These things are best avoided in Tokyo.

DISOBEYING RULES

Even though Japanese people usually overlook the *faux pas* of unwitting tourists, you can score brownie points by taking certain rules to heart. These include not stepping on tatami mats with your street shoes on – take off your shoes at the door! Also, do not wear your house slippers to the toilet – there are special bathroom slippers placed there for that purpose. And when you leave the toilet, don't forget to replace the slippers with the heels facing the door. Don't take any soap with you into the hot water pools at an onsen. These pools are meant for relaxing, and you should only enter once you are completely clean! Don't stick your chopsticks in your rice bowl – this is only done at funerals. Don't shout or talk loudly – you will seldom achieve the desired result.

MISINTERPRETING A YES

When Japanese people say *"hai"*, it does mean yes, and it sounds like agreement – however, it might also mean the opposite. They often simply mean "Keep talking – I'm listening". They will seldom express a direct no *(iie)*, as this might be hurtful.

BE CAUTIOUS

In nightlife districts like Roppongi and Kabukichō, never let your drink out of your sight. Criminals might replace it with drugs. In hostess clubs, be sure to keep track of the costs so that you don't get bamboozled.

AVOID TRAVELLING AT THE WRONG TIME

At New Year's, during the "Golden Week" (between 29 April and 6 May) as well as on the days surrounding the Buddhist Festival of the Dead in mid-August, half of Japan is on the move. At these times, all excursion destinations are overfilled and the prices are significantly higher.

DON`T FORGET A GIFT FOR YOUR HOST

Never visit someone without a gift! Ideally, this should be a small, attractive gift from your home country. If you want to buy a gift yourself in Tokyo, do so at a well-known department store. Have it wrapped there, and present it this way as a sign of its prestigious origin.

DON`T PANIC DURING EARTHQUAKES

Perceptible tremors occur in Japan over one thousand times per year – but real shaking only starts at Level 3 on the seven-point Japanese scale. Most important: don't panic, and keep an eye on the situation. Extinguish any open fires immediately, turn off the gas tap and open windows and doors. Do not run outside! In case of a serious quake, seek shelter – ideally under a steel door frame – and pay attention to radio and television announcements. In Tokyo, there are many meeting points for residents after strong earthquakes where the authorities can look after the people. Follow Tokyo residents to one of these.